High Performance Gymnastics

EDITED BY

Laurita Marconi Schiavon, PhD
State University of São Paulo
Biosciences Institute
Rio Claro, BRAZIL

Thomas Heinen, PhD
University of Hildesheim
Institute of Sport Science
Hildesheim, GERMANY

Marco Antonio Coelho Bortoleto, PhD
University of Campinas
Physical Education Faculty
Campinas, BRAZIL

Myrian Nunomura, PhD
University of São Paulo
School of Physical Education and Sport
Ribeirão Preto Campus, BRAZIL

Eliana de Toledo, PhD
University of Campinas
College of Applied Sciences
Limeira, BRAZIL

Bibliografische Information der Deutschen Nationalbibliothek
Die Deutsche Bibliothek verzeichnet diese Publikation in der Deutschen Nationalbibliografie; detaillierte bibliografische Daten sind im Internet über http://dnb.ddb.de abrufbar.

© 2014 Arete Verlag Christian Becker, Hildesheim.
www.arete-verlag.de

Das Werk und seine Teile sind urheberrechtlich geschützt. Jede Nutzung in anderen als den gesetzlich zugelassenen Fällen bedarf der vorherigen schriftlichen Einwilligung des Verlages. Dies gilt auch und insbesondere für Vervielfältigungen, Übersetzungen, Verfilmungen und die Einspeicherung sowie Datenvorhaltung in elektronischen und digitalen Systemen.

Druck und Verarbeitung: CPI GmbH, Birkach.
ISBN 978-3-942468-30-5

Acknowledgment:
This book is dedicated to all those who have contributed and who still contribute to the development of competitive gymnastics. A special credit is given to the coaches, who, with a lot of effort, study and bravery, face numerous challenges, and do their best to advance gymnastics.

Cover design: Marco Fontanetti.

Last but not least, we thank the former Brazilian gymnast Luisa Parente for providing photos from a travelling exhibition on her life.

THIS PUBLICATION IS GRATEFUL FOR THE INSTITUTIONAL
SUPPORT RECEIVED BY INBRADE

INSTITUTO BRASILEIRO
DE DESENVOLVIMENTO
DO ESPORTE
BRAZILIAN INSTITUTE OF SPORT DEVELOPMENT

GRADUATE COURSES
IMPROVEMENT COURSES
SPORTS CONSULTING

WWW.INBRADE.COM

Contents

Foreword by Ivan Čuk		i
Foreword by Hardy Fink		iv
Preface		vii
1	Gymnastics challenges – a view from 50 years of coaching and teaching - *Keith Russell*	1
2	The group in rhythmic gymnastics - *Márcia Regina Aversani Lourenço & Ieda Parra Barbosa Rinaldi*	19
3	Profile, motivations, and the challenges of artistic gymnastics coaches in Brazil - *Myrian Nunomura & Mauricio Santos Oliveira*	41
4	Contributions of sport psychology to competitive gymnastics - *Thomas Heinen, Pia M. Vinken & Konstantinos Velentzas*	65
5	The content of rhythmic gymnastics routines *Lurdes Ávila-Carvalho, Catarina Leandro & Eunice Lebre*	81
6	Qualitative video analysis as a pedagogical tool in artistic gymnastics - *Marco Antonio Coelho Bortoleto & César Jose Duarte Peixoto*	99
7	Gymnastics: a game of rules - *Jean-François Robin*	117
8	Portraits of high performance rhythmic gymnastics in Brazil - analysis and proposals - *Eliana de Toledo & Kizzy Fernandes Antualpa*	137
9	Gymnastics coaching and science: biomechanics perspectives - *Gareth Irwin, Geneviève K. R. Williams & David G. Kerwin*	163
10	Reflections on planning and control of sport training in rhythmic gymnastics. - *Mélix I. Avilés, Yolaini Govea Díaz & Nelly Ochoa Borrás*	177
11	Psychological aspects in the sport preparation of brazilian female gymnasts participating in the Olympic Games: the gymnasts' view - *Laurita Marconi Schiavon*	195
Author's biographies (in alphabetical order)		225

Foreword by Ivan Čuk

Editor-in-Chief of Science of Gymnastics Journal

SIGARC symposium in Brazil was up to now hold three times. For 2012, experts from all over the world were invited who prepared scientific presentations as well as book chapters from the field of their expertise. In this book there are eleven chapters of excellent readings for coaches, gymnasts, judges, physical education teachers, students, and even parents of gymnasts, and of course, scientists, who will continue to improve and extend gymnastics knowledge. Whether authors are dealing with artistic or rhythmic gymnastics, from my point of view, both sides are interesting since they are focusing on general aspects, which are always of high interests for all gymnastics disciplines.

The first chapter was prepared by the FIG's scientific commission president Keith Russell, dealing with a mostly philosophical overview of half a century development of gymnastics. The most important medical conclusion was that gymnastics does not hamper gymnast's growth, which is something that envy sport researchers and medicine people claimed for decades and thus made a lot of negative propaganda against gymnastics. Márcia Regina Aversani Lourenço and Ieda Parra Barbosa Rinaldi prepared the second chapter, covering their expertise on group exercises in rhythmic gymnastics, where the most important topics are different changes of formations (collaboration and communication between gymnasts), without losing individual object manipulation technique mastery. Myrian Nunomura and Mauricio Santos Oliveira were exploring profiles and the motivation of artistic gymnastics coaches in Brazil. Their most valuable conclusion is that universities can be of great support for coaches, thus making the coaching process in gymnastics friendly, injury safe and with high achievements. Thomas Heinen, Pia Vinken and Konstantinos Velentzas discuss the contribution of sport psychology to competitive gymnastics. They stated that experienced gymnasts are far from being 'machines' that produce the same pattern of movement in every trial. It was concluded, that in order to make every trial as stable as possible, psychologists can assist them. Lurdes Ávila-Carvalho, Catarina Leandro and Eunice Lebre were researching the content of competition routines in rhythmic gymnastics. According to their analysis of articles they suggest new studies in the area of execution, and some changes in the Code of Points. Marco Antonio Coelho Bortoleto and César Jose Peixoto Duarte made a review of qualitative video analysis as a pedagogical tool in artistic gymnastics. The important conclusion thereby is that operating video hardware and software should also be a part of the knowledge offered in coaches' education programs, perhaps as a first step prior to discussing biomechanical studies. Jean-François Robin made a philosophical approach towards gymnastics whilst defining gymnastics as a game of rules. Among these rules are "difficulty" and "execution", like Jing and Jang, which generate basic strategies how to win at competition. Eliana de Toledo and Kizzy Fernandes Antualpa present an in-detail overview of high performance rhythmic gymnastics in Brazil, thereby discussing aspects such as Brazilian participation in the Olympic Games, and also highlighting potential aspects that could help to develop rhythmic gymnastics in the future. Gareth Irwin, Geneviève Williams, and David Kerwin refer to gymnastics coaches and biomechanics perspectives, where highly complex skills demand extra knowledge from coaches in order to prepare proper conditioning, proper skill development, and learning. Mélix Ilisástigui Avilés, Yolaini Govea Díaz, and Nelly Ochoa Borrás deal with planning of sport training in rhythmic gymnastics. The authors discuss some interesting limits when the training was efficient according to coaches plans. The last chapter was written by Laurita Marconi Schiavon on psychological aspects in the sport preparation of female Brazilian gymnasts participating in the Olympic Games. Her work shows the importance of interviews with gymnasts, and how important it is to analyze past work in a frame of future activities.

Brazil is preparing for the Olympic Games in Rio de Janeiro in 2016; they are improving not only facilities for the games, but what is most important, they are maintaining and developing 'know how' in order to work with athletes to be successful. Results at the 2012 Olympic Games and the 2013 World Championships speak for themselves. This book will have -after Rio 2016- still important knowledge from which all participants in gymnastics can gain.

Ljubljana, October 2013.
Ivan Čuk

Foreword by Hardy Fink

Director, FIG Education & Academy Programs

These proceedings from the 2012 SIGARC symposium encompasses a broad range of historical, empirical, and scientific articles presented by some of the world's leading practitioners and researchers in the area of gymnastics. This symposium featured presentations about the various gymnastics sports, and with focused research on rhythmic-, men's- and women's-gymnastics from biomechanical, psychological, planning, and methodological perspectives.

The introductory presentation by Russell takes a critical and enlightening look at all of the gymnastics sports from the insights he gained over a lifetime of coaching and teaching gymnastics. He also dispels forcefully the suggestion that gymnastics participation "retards" growth.

Four papers discuss aspects of rhythmic gymnastics. The beauty and the challenges related to group rhythmic performances from the experiences of the Brazil group are presented by Lourenço et al. The content of rhythmic gymnastics routines are analyzed with reference to Code of Points requirements by Ávila-Carvalho et al. A third paper, this one by Avilés et al, studies the principles of periodization, planning, and pedagogy applied to training in rhythmic gymnastics. The fourth paper by Toledo and Antualpa deals with the development of high performance rhythmic gymnastics in Brazil as well as Brazilian participation in international competitions.

Psychology applied to gymnastics training is also presented in three different papers. Nunomura and Oliveira look at the difficult and essential tasks of coaches in artistic gymnastics by presenting data on coaches' profiles and motivation. Heinen et al. outline how sport psychology can contribute to gymnastics performances from the analysis of the performance demands, psychological profiles, and psychological interventions. Schiavon takes a fascinating look at psychological aspects of preparing gymnastics teams and specifically the Brazilian women's team for the Olympics.

Other sport sciences are not ignored. Irwin et al. look at biomechanical analysis and how this science can enhance the effectiveness of gymnastics coaches. Bortoleto and Duarte take a different but equally enlightening approach. It is that of qualitative video analysis that can be quickly and easily meaningful to a coach instead of the sometimes more difficult to understand biomechanical and quantitative analysis.

Finally, no overview of gymnastics would be complete without the regulations that attempt to direct and guide its direction. Robin presents the influence of the Code of Points on gymnasts, coaches, and judges.

The totality of these proceedings from the 2012 SIGARC symposium provides a large amount of scientific, pedagogical, methodological, empirical and experiential information that can be of benefit to every gymnastics coach. Even the best or most successful of coaches can improve – can be better – by knowing and incorporating the information provided.

Moreover, every book that presents the content and philosophy of the systematic, careful, and informed coaching of athletes is a welcome addition to gymnastics. And for this reason, I very much appreciate that this book will help improve our sports for all participants, but most especially for the gymnasts.

Canada/Switzerland, December 2013.
Hardy Fink

Preface by the Editors

Laurita Marconi Schiavon, Thomas Heinen, Marco Antonio Coelho Bortoleto, Myrian Nunomura & Eliana de Toledo

The book "High Performance Gymnastics" arises from a partnership among the three State Universities of São Paulo (UNICAMP, UNESP, USP), and the University of Hildesheim (Germany). This experience has arisen due to the interest of many students, professionals, and researchers in gymnastics, who are looking for new scientific and pedagogical approaches that would contribute to its development. After three editions of the International Seminar on Competitive Artistic and Rhythmic Gymnastics (SIGARC), we have seen an opportunity to collaborate in producing the book presented herein.

Among the many issues addressed directly and indirectly in this book, biomechanics of gymnastics is the core theme of the chapter of Gareth Irwin, Geneviève Williams, and David Kerwin (Cardiff Metropolitan University), as well as the chapter of Marco A. C. Bortoleto and César Peixoto, which is the outcome of a partnership between Brazil (UNICAMP) and Portugal (Lisbon Technical University).

Psychological aspects in dealing with gymnasts are addressed in two chapters. The first one was authored by Thomas Heinen (University of Hildesheim), Pia Vinken (Leibniz University Hanover) and Konstantinos Velentzas (Bielefeld University). The other chapter was written by Laurita Marconi Schiavon (UNESP), presenting proposals for intervention and the experiences from major Brazilian Olympic gymnasts.

The Brazilian context in the field of rhythmic gymnastics is analyzed by Eliana de Toledo (UNICAMP) and Kizzy Antualpa (Metrocamp), revealing the scenario of the rhythmic gymnastics; and also by Myrian Nunomura (USP) and Mauricio Oliveira (UFES), discussing the profile, motivations and challenges of artistic gymnastics coaches in the country.

The routines composition analysis, planning and training control of rhythmic gymnasts are also topics covered by Márcia Aversani Lourenço (UNOPAR) and Ieda Parra Barbosa Rinaldi (UEM), focusing on the particularities of "group". Lurdes Ávila-Carvalho (UP), Catarina Leandro (ULP) and Eunice Lebre (UP) discuss on the competitive exercises in the rhythmic gymnastics routines. Mélix Avilés, Yolaini Diaz, and Nelly Borrás (UCCFD) address the periodization and training control in rhythmic gymnastics.

In a broader approach, the process and the principles of high performance training in gymnastics are discussed by Keith Russell (University of Saskatchewan) in the first chapter of this book, covering the

Preface by the Editors. ix

outcome of more than 50 years' experience in this sport. This comprehensive look on gymnastics guides the analysis of Jean François Robin (INSEP), who proposes a reflection on the social history that surrounds the rules of gymnastics, as well as their consequences for the better understanding of this phenomenon.

We believe that the contributions presented in this book stand for important advancements in the academic and scientific environment of our field. In this context, this book aims to build a new space for reflection, sharing knowledge, disseminating innovation, and technology, as well as joining authors from eight different nationalities, thus becoming an important source of knowledge in competitive gymnastics.

Finally, dear fellow academics, coaches, gymnasts, judges, researchers, and others involved with gymnastics, we hope you all enjoy the reading! - Gymnastics greetings!

Brazil/Germany, February 2014.
Laurita Marconi Schiavon
Thomas Heinen
Marco Antonio Coelho Bortoleto
Myrian Nunomura
Eliana de Toledo

CHAPTER 1

GYMNASTICS CHALLENGES - A VIEW FROM 50 YEARS OF COACHING AND TEACHING

Keith Russell

University of Saskatchewan - College of Kinesiology (Canada).
Correspondence to: keith.russell@usask.ca

Acknowledgement:
The author would like to thank Mr. Hardy Fink and Dr. John Atkinson for reading and offering suggestions and corrections during the preparation of this essay.

1.1 Introduction

While watching the recent Olympics I continued to marvel at the extremely high level of athletic prowess shown by gymnasts. They are surely the most superb athletes. Their power, strength and flexibility set the world standards, and the complexity and number of skills they must perform surpass what most other athletes must attempt. In addition, gymnasts must overcome fear while, at the same time, they must satisfy the requirements for artistry. The Olympic family of gymnastics sports (artistic gymnastics, trampoline gymnastics, rhythmic gymnastics) is certainly at the very cutting edge of athletic achievement. This is, of course, also true for the non-Olympic gymnastics sports of acrobatic gymnastics and aerobic gymnastics.

My first intention with this brief essay is to recognize these amazing achievements and marvel at the journey gymnastics is taking. Gymnastics sports appear to be evolving much faster than other sports. The skills that are currently being performed by pre-teen gymnasts all over the world are more difficult and more complex than those done by Olympic champions only a few years ago. Almost every apparatus has had radical structural enhancements resulting in profound changes in the skills performed (think of sprung floors, padded beams, sprung and padded vault tables, coil springs on vaulting boards, smaller rails on asymmetric and parallel bars that are now made of hollow, springy fiberglass). If you look at other sports, you will see slow incremental changes over time rather than the rapid, multiple and significant changes in gymnastics sports (the notable exception of the fiberglass pole in athletics produced a similar revolutionary change in that sport).

The family of gymnastics sports is also rapidly evolving into new variants. Trampoline gained Olympic inclusion at a very young age and the quickly expanding sport of aerobic gymnastics is evolving with brand new forms being competed at World Championships. Popularity and growth brings new challenges and thus the second intention of this article is to highlight some of these new challenges and openly posit some possible solutions.

1.2 Challenges from outside: circuses and new sports related to gymnastics

Recently gymnasts from several sports have gained new opportunities to continue in a performance role after retirement from their sport. This is due to the expanding popularity of circuses around the world. Indeed, these opportunities have put considerable pressure on several gymnastics sports whose coaches and athletes are migrating out of the sports and into the circus as performers or coaches. In my country alone more than 30 top coaches have left gymnastics jobs for circus jobs. Acrobatic gymnastics, in particular, has been adversely affected by this trend and it is only recently that the circus community has begun to realize that without coaches in gymnastics clubs, their supply of acrobats will dry up. There are now several initiatives addressing this problem but the challenge remains to keep coaches and athletes in the sports, when there is pressure to leave and join the circus.

There is also the emerging challenge of how to accommodate and cooperate with other forms of gymnastics and acrobatic activities such as 'TeamGym' and 'cheerleading' which are also thriving and expanding and are putting pressures on the established gymnastics sports for athletes, coaches and facilities. Federations that embrace these emerging sports can find themselves overwhelmed with new members and the subsequent political pressure to share resources. While this is not an unhealthy trend, it compounds the challenge to attract and keep gymnasts in the Olympic sports.

1.3 Challenges from outside: the changing opinions about gymnastics

As part of my professional functions within the FIG I have the privilege of presenting lectures to the Coach Education Academies and to various special topic seminars and conferences. On several occasions I have given a lecture entitled "From Paragon to Pariah" in which I trace the changes in perceptions that the scientific and medical community has towards competitive gymnastics over the past 50 years. I relate that when I was a young coach / science student, the dominant view was that gymnastics was the paragon of sports. It was healthy, artistic, wholesome, and the foundation of physical education. That is no longer the dominant opinion in the scientific, educational or medical community.

Instead of the paragon, gymnastics is becoming more of a pariah sport. Now it is just as often considered to be an example of excessive (even abusive) coaching practices, cheating judges, and catastrophic accidents. Books such as *Little Girls in Pretty Boxes* (1995, 2000, Joan Ryan), *Off Balance • A Memoir* (2012, Dominique Moceanu), or *The Unfree Exercise* (2013, Simone Heitinga & Stasja Kohler) have added grist for the mill of discontent. Issues raised in these books are also discussed in the FIG Coach Education Academies as well as in the inner circles of gymnastics leadership, but there remains much to do about solving some of the problems.

Gymnastics challenges.

So what has changed in the journey from paragon to pariah? Obviously, the sports of gymnastics have changed. The following are some of the concerns that I think have to be addressed to return gymnastics to its paragon status.

1.4 Challenges from inside: safety and injuries

With regard to the safety of gymnastics sports, there is a dearth of comprehensive data available on injury epidemiology. There are many single-case studies and case-series studies published but there are very few broadly based studies that allow comparison to other sports. To add to the confusion, different studies report a wide range of results from gymnastics sports (often the specific sport is not even identified) having high injuries per thousand hours of training to having low injury rates per thousand hours of training (this is known as incidence rate). What is needed is a systematic study, or series of studies, comparing high performance gymnasts from several countries and from several gymnastics sports, to determine injury incidence rates and patterns of injuries. Similarly, the incidence rates of catastrophic injuries in gymnastics sports is virtually unknown. There is no central database to track any types of injuries and to determine how prevalent they are relative to other sports.

This vacuum of data is particularly shameful with respect to injuries that have occurred in major international competitions and exhibitions under the auspices of the international governing body. The scientific and medical communities do not even know the prevalence (total numbers) of injuries sustained in training before competition, or during major competitions. Do certain apparatus, or certain skills, or certain sports, account for more injuries? Do certain skill combinations endanger athletes more than others? Do certain ages or morphologies suffer more injuries or different types of injuries? Do new innovations in apparatus design increase or decrease injury prevalence, incidence, and severity? Are there different injury patterns for males and females? Many questions need answering and the collection, analysis and publication of medical injury data from both competitions and training is long, long overdue.

1.5 Challenges from inside: rules and judging

In general, gymnastics sports have both the privilege and the curse of being subjectively evaluated. In addition to technical subjectivity, there is also the slippery issue of subjectively evaluating artistic merit. In order to decrease the subjectivity, the sports try to objectify their evaluation, and the more they try, the more complex become the rules. Yet without objective evaluation we can easily have nationalistic biases that are very difficult to contain. To add to the problem - those who judge are different from those who coach. It has been my experience over 50 years that the subsets of 'judges' and 'coaches' are very different. The more mathematical approach of many judges differs from the more technical, artistic approach of many coaches. But, those who judge determine the rules.

It has long been the case that a small cadre of judges has dictated rules in gymnastic sports. Indeed it was only recently that FIG mandated that coaches, or at least judges educated as coaches, be part of their international technical committees. This occurred as a result of the FIG coach education academies being developed and rules put in place ensuring that all judges wanting to be elected to technical committees must have passed their level 3 FIG coach education licence in that sport. This is a good step in the right direction and hopefully, over time, this will result in more gymnast / coach centered rules and regulations. Now two things need to happen: simplified rules / scoring that the public can easily comprehend, and rules that more closely align with the opinions of the coaches and the scientific / medical community.

The FIG has recently initiated a series of seminars in an attempt to standardize the Code of Points of the various sports. There were large differences in how the various sports evaluated their athletes and these differences were becoming ever more disparate. Hopefully there will soon be greater unanimity between sports. But the following trends remain to be dealt with:

1. The rules / codes are too complex, too deductive, too mathematical.

2. The requirements and rewards for creativity / artistry have been sacrificed for the more easily measured acrobatic elements. This has led to complexity in acrobatic content that is often impossible for spectators (and some judges) to differentiate. Can spectators differentiate between double twisting double somersault and a triple twisting double somersault, or Endo circles done in el grip versus under grip?

3. In an attempt to offset the inherent biases in subjective evaluations, the size of officials' panels in several gymnastics sports has increased in size to comically large numbers.

1.6 Changes needed from inside: artistic gymnastics

Artistic gymnasts are the most superbly conditioned of all Olympic athletes and demonstrate the highest level of skilled human movement. The magnitude of biological loads experienced in artistic gymnastics is at the limits of human tissue tolerance and injuries caused by overuse and by insufficient recovery is a pressing problem. Because of the early specialization of women's artistic gymnastics (WAG), and to a lesser extent men's artistic gymnastics (MAG), growth plate injuries are of particular concern. There is limited, but compelling research, to indicate that this problem is getting worse.

Skill convergence has exacerbated the overuse injury problem in WAG. Female Artistic gymnasts now do basically the same tumbling skills on floor, vault, and beam with only bars presenting different movement patterns. At the same time, the training hours per week have been increasing and are now at levels that many scientists and medical personnel consider excessive. This results in female artistic gymnasts doing more and more repetitions, of fewer and fewer movement patterns, which inevitably leads to overuse injuries.

Previously there was the phenomenon of younger and younger females becoming champions. The 1976 Olympics saw the emergence of the 14 year old Olympic medalist Nadia Comaneci. With recent Olympic rule changes limiting gymnastics participants to only those 16 years or older, it would appear that this problem is solved. However, even though average ages of female artistic gymnasts have steadily increased over the past 10 years, the height and weight of Olympic WAG athletes have stayed much the same. Since later maturity correlates with shorter stature, does this mean that we now have females who are even later maturing than was previously? It could be the case that we are now inadvertently selecting very late maturing females.

It seems obvious that the solution to this problem is to change the rules to minimize the current advantage enjoyed by small stature females. Increase artistry, decrease acrobatics, reward execution more generously, and decrease the emphasis on difficulty. Female artistic gymnasts could develop at a slower pace, eliminating the need for such intensive training before puberty. We know that the biological age when gymnasts are most vulnerable to growth plate injuries coincides with the time they are now training hardest. We know that skill trends and skill combinations that are required in the international rules can be harmful to growing tissues. We know that the adult female is greatly disadvantaged in WAG. We know that the necessity for 'sticking' landings, combined with the hardness of international landing mats is the genesis of many injuries. All these issues can be addressed by rule changes.

There is even a persistent assumption in scientific and medical publications that participation in WAG stunts growth or alters growth. But there is also a contrary opinion, also based on research, that states there is no evidence that this phenomenon exists. To address this difference, the top eight experts in the world - four from each side of the argument - were invited to a two day colloquium in Lausanne in February of 2011 to debate the following questions and come up with a position / consensus paper:

1. Is there a negative effect of training on attained adult stature?

2. Is there a negative effect of training on growth of body segments?

3. Does training function to attenuate pubertal growth and maturation, specifically rate of growth and the timing and tempo of maturation?

4. Does training have a negative influence on the endocrine system?

This expert group carefully analyzed every paper written on this subject and their consensus opinion was published recently with the following conclusions (Malina, Baxter-Jones, Armstrong et al., 2013):

1. Adult height or near adult height of female and male artistic gymnasts is not compromised by intensive gymnastics training.

2. Gymnastics training does not appear to attenuate growth of upper (sitting height) or lower (legs) body segment lengths.

3. Gymnastics training does not appear to attenuate pubertal growth and maturation, neither rate of growth nor the timing and tempo of the growth spurt.

4. Available data are inadequate to address the issue of intensive gymnastics training and alterations within the endocrine system.

All studies claiming that there was evidence of stunted or deflected growth were shown to be either statistically flawed or design flawed. The group also expressed concern with inappropriate nomenclature used in many published papers (Malina, Baxter-Jones, Armstrong et al., 2013, pp. 795-796):

> "Care in using terminology implying a causative link between gymnastics training and growth and maturation status is warranted. Examples include adversely affected, blunted growth, growth faltering, without a normal growth spurt, inhibited growth, attenuated growth, deterioration in growth, growth deficits, among others."

As an example of this continuing use of inappropriate terminology take note of the conclusion of a recent paper published in a medical journal (Georgopoulos, Theodoropoulou, Roupas et al., 2012):

Gymnastics challenges.

> "Although in elite RG genetic predisposition for growth was fully preserved, in elite female AG final adult height falls shorter than genetically determined target height, though still within the standard error of prediction" (p. 68).

The researchers' statement that target heights are within the standard error of prediction is stating that there is no statistical proof of any effect. But in the very next sentence they state:

> "Although this slight impairment of growth remains well within the normal limits..." (p. 68).

How can there be an "impairment in growth", if growth was shown to be normal? - There is still much research needed in this area, but there is no credible evidence to date to show any detrimental effects of gymnastics training on growth.

Men's artistic gymnastics, though not so hotly researched, is not without its problems. The many injuries to wrists and shoulders in MAG could be reduced by rule changes. Some small steps have been taken in the most recent Code of Points, but more could still be done. The spectacular increase in difficulty in MAG has put huge strains on the capacity of coaches to continue to hold boys in the sport. Again, a possible solution is to reward more artistry, execution, finesse, and originality rather than the easy-to-judge 'difficulty'. Alternatives such as 'TeamGym', 'cheerleading', and other gymnastics sports are very attractive to young males who cannot train 30 plus hours per week for 10 or 15 years now needed in MAG.

1.7 Changes needed from inside: rhythmic gymnastics

This sport should truly be called 'artistic gymnastics'. Here the marriage of skill and artistry is the most complete and the potential for expansion of this art form is huge. However, the continued trend towards contortionism, though slightly abated, not only limits high performers to a narrow subset of genetically hypermobile individuals, but it also results in injury to those youngsters who are not genetically hypermobile, but who train as if they were. Back injuries continue to be a factor in the sport and there does not seem to be a political will to address this problem.

Recent updates to the nomenclature and categorization of skills should encourage better understanding of the sport outside its relatively small circle of insiders. This improvement will also allow for more universal biomechanical / anatomical / taxonomical discussions to occur amongst similar artistic sports and sport scientists.

Due to coaching perceptions and intractable training philosophies, rhythmic gymnasts do not train sufficiently for power development. The fear of hypertrophy seems to smother experimentation in non-hyper-trophy-inducing power training methods that could improve the dynamics of the sport. There is the perception, to the non-expert, that rhythmic gymnasts perform almost identical routines but simply change the hand apparatus. This perception could be reduced by rules that encourage very different movement patterns, specific to each apparatus. This would also help with the overuse injury problems since the training would then be much more variable.

The sport would greatly benefit from a broadened participant base, a reduction in its dependence on hypermobility and greater global distribution of winners. The trend to glitzier leotards and extravagant glittery makeup does not engender rhythmic gymnastics to the international sports press nor to many spectators. And finally, there is the problem of judging which, if not soon fixed, will reduce this sport to irrelevance.

1.8 The oldest discipline and its challenges: acrobatic gymnastics

Here is a wonderfully creative, exciting sport that is smothering itself in complexity and judging incomprehension. Of all the gymnastics sports, this is the oldest and when observing its offshoots in the entertainment world, it should be the most watched. But instead, it remains rather obscure. The sport would benefit from a simplified competitive structure, simplified rules, and sticking to its acrobatic heritage rather than attempting to be partly dance, partly tumbling, partly figure skating.

There is potential to combine it with other gymnastics sports to make a more universally appealing product. Aerobic gymnastics and cheerleading both have strong elements of acrobatics but lack the safety, technical expertise, skill level and long history of acrobatic gymnastics. It seems plausible that some marriage of these should be explored, especially since aerobic gymnastics is adding more and more acrobatics. Alternatively, acrobatic gymnastics itself could go through some fundamental restructuring.

1.9 The emerging disciplines and their challenges: trampoline gymnastics

This is the youngest of all gymnastics disciplines and already it has Olympic status. The relative simplicity (one apparatus) of the sport of trampoline compared to the other gymnastics sports is clearly contributing to its spectator appeal. Its success should set an example to other gymnastics sports that could reduce their complexity at no loss in spectator appeal.

While insufficient physical preparation was endemic in the past, better coach education by FIG is changing this. It would be desirable to have research on the long term effects of trampoline training on stress incontinence and related tissue changes due to repeated rapid deceleration / acceleration especially in light of the new rule to measure jump height (time in the air) that is now factored into the gymnast's score. There is the possibility, seen in MAG and WAG, that more air time will simply lead to more somersaults and twists and more spectacular falls, rather than more artistry and better execution. The initial results of this rule change, however, seem to point to more improvements than negative outcomes. This young sport, while a little unidimensional in its Olympic format, makes a wonderful spectator event when joined by its sister, but non-Olympic disciplines, of synchronized trampoline, tumbling, and double mini trampoline.

1.10 The emerging disciplines and their challenges: aerobic gymnastics

This sport is having a surge in popularity and the FIG's involvement over the past 10 years has really helped it grow internationally. It has suffered, as an elite sport, from a somewhat unsophisticated coaching ethos, but that is rapidly changing with the FIG academy program. It is evolving rapidly, gaining participants steadily and has the potential to be a very exciting international sport. It could, however, also become a spectacle of many fitness exhibitions and never really attain true elite sport status. The latter may already be the trend, as shown by the introduction of the two new disciplines of 'step' and 'dance' in the past World Championships. But greater levels of participation and more spectacular exhibitions are not necessarily bad, as witnessed in the next, and by far the largest, branch of FIG's family.

1.11 The stalwart: gymnastics for All

By far the largest group of gymnastics devotees is collectively called 'gymnastics for all'. These are the participants of educational and recreational gymnastics, gymnastics festivals, mass displays of gymnastics, and fitness / social gymnastics clubs. For the most part, these are non-competitive forms of gymnastics done for fun, fitness, fundamentals and friendship. Traditionally these forms of gymnastics were practiced mainly in Europe, but there is now a large following in Asia and increasingly in Africa and the Americas. The role of the FIG has been to coordinate, organize and publicize the major festivals that showcase the myriad forms of gymnastics for all. The premier event is the quadrennial World Gymnaestrada but there is also a newly minted competition for group (club) performance world supremacy. As an example of life-long healthy participation, gymnastics for all remains the 'paragon' amongst sports. What other sport can boast such a large participatory, non-competitive, global mass of young and old participants engaged in so many activities, all with the common thread of gymnastics movement? But gymnastics for all should beware of introducing too much competition and losing their distinctiveness and their raison d'etre. And, like many of the other sports under FIG's umbrella, gymnastics for all would greatly benefit by increasing its support for, and use of, the coaching education academies (foundations level).

1.12 The missing link

The one area that FIG has not embraced to the same extent as many other international sport governing organizations is support for, and celebration of, athletes with physical and mental challenges. While there are a few countries encouraging the inclusion of these athletes in special competitions, FIG has not yet taken on this challenge with any enthusiasm.

1.13 My conclusion

From the vantage point of 50 years participating in gymnastics, I would like to conclude: the gymnastics family of sports and activities is flourishing and expanding and is increasingly more exciting and dynamic. What problems there are, can be fixed. FIG's elected, appointed and hired leaders are working under strong leadership to educate, to change, and to clean up those aspects of the sports that are less than desirable. The 3000 year journey continues to somersault and spring into exciting celebrations of art and sport.

References

Georgopoulos, N., Theodoropoulou, A., Roupas, N., Rottstein, L., Tsekouras, A., Mylonas, P., Vagenakis, G., Koukkou, E., Armeni, A., Sakellaropoulos, G., Leglise, M., Vagenakis, A., & Markou, K. (2012). Growth velocity and final height in elite female rhythmic and artistic gymnasts. *Hormones, 11*(1), 61-69.

Heitinga, S., & Kohler, S. (2013). *De onvrije oefening*. [The unfree exercise]. Geus: De Uitgeverij.

Malina, R. M., Baxter-Jones, A. D., Armstrong, N., Beunen, G. P. , Caine, D., Daly, R. M., Lewis, R. D., Rogol, A. D., & Russell, K. (2013). Role of intensive training in the growth and maturation of artistic gymnasts. *Sports Medicine, 43*(9), 783-802.

Moceanu, D. (2012). *Off balance. A Memoir.* New York, NY: Touchstone.

Ryan, J. (1995, 2000). *Little girls in pretty boxes. The making and breaking of elite gymnasts and figure skaters.* New York, NY: Warner Books, Inc.

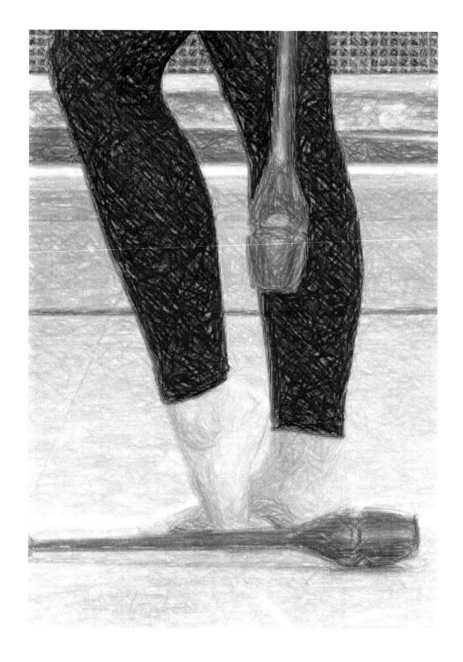

CHAPTER 2

THE GROUP IN RHYTHMIC GYMNASTICS

Márcia Regina Aversani Lourenço[1] & Ieda Parra Barbosa Rinaldi[2]

[1] *University of Northern Paraná (Brazil).*
Correspondence to: marcia.aversani@sercomtel.com.br

[2] *State University of Maringá - Department of Physical Education (Brazil).*
Correspondence to: parrarinaldi@hotmail.com

2.1 Introduction

Rhythmic gymnastics is an individual and group Olympic sport, which has a great number of practitioners in Brazil. Working on the group dynamics of this sport is no easy task, since training must be organized in a way that engages the interest of the group so that they want to work as a team towards a common result: together as a group, one for all and all for one! Everything in the group dynamics is intense, choosing a music that everyone likes, selecting body and/or apparatus difficulties that all the group members can perform without mistakes, creating changes and collaborations whilst knowing exactly who is going to perform the more difficult elements at risky moments, realizing who is capable of throwing two or more apparatus at the same time, and additionally, in order to decide on the style of the leotard and the apparatus colors it is necessary to listen to everyones' opinion. Besides all the aspects just mentioned, in-depth training of the executions need to be extremely synchronized.

The group coach must also remain separate, since leadership is very important, and in order to avoid losing focus, it is necessary to invigorate the energy of the group every day, because if one of the gymnasts is not okay then there is a risk of training not happening and good united training makes the difference in competitions. Training a group of gymnasts that exhibit different potential and difficulties requires specific knowledge from the coach, like detailed planning which creates the opportunity of transforming these differences into positive results without putting all the components of the training aside.

Rhythmic gymnastics has been included in the Olympic Games since 1984, when the first individual competition took place in Los

Angeles, although it was in Atlanta in 1996 that the group sport became part of the Olympic competitions. On that occasion, nine teams participated in the group competition, seven from European nations, and one from Asia plus the host country. The Sydney Olympic Games had ten nations in the group competition, nine vacancies were filled from the pre-Olympic competition and the final one went to the American champions, in this case, Brazil (Santos, Lourenço, & Gaio, 2010).

In 2004, ten teams participated in the group competition, all of them, including the Brazilian squad, were selected during the pre-Olympics, which took place a year before in Budapest. At the Olympic Games in Beijing in 2008, the number of teams, who always attract a lot of public support, was raised to twelve nations with vacancies for ten in the Pre-Olympics at Patras (2007). The remaining vacancies were filled by the continents without representatives in the top positions. Brazil, once again, represented the American continent (Santos et al., 2010).

The classification system for the twelve spots at the Olympic Games in London started in the Moscow World Championships in 2010, organized by the International Gymnastic Federation (FIG), with the participation of 29 countries. Of these 29 nations, 24 were selected for the pre-Olympics which took place in the French city of Montpellier (2011). There, only six countries achieved a place in the Olympics. Four spots were allocated at the test event in London at the start of 2012 and the balance was filled by one nation from each continent with no representatives plus the host country. In this cycle Canada was the representative for the American continent. The test event has started to be more important in all the gymnastic disciplines as the remaining Olympic places are awarded at this event which took place in the same year as the Games. The expectation for the 2016 Olympic Games in Rio de Janeiro is to keep the same classification system for the rhythmic gymnastics groups.

In Brazil there is a lot of good group work and in rhythmic gymnastics there have been impressive results: Brazil competed in three of the Olympic Games and in two of them as a finalist. The first national championships took place in the 1970's, but it is known that the introduction of this discipline in Brazil took place approximately twenty years before with the arrival of the Hungarian teacher Ilona Peuker to Rio de Janeiro. She utilized instruments of Brazilian folklore in her choreographies, such as coconut shells and tambourines. Ilona also created the Gymnasts United Group (GUG) which participated in regional, national and international competitions and also helped in the dissemination of the sport in several regions of the country. In 1975, Ilona Peuker ended her professional activities, participating in the VIth Gymnaestrada, at Berlin with the members of the GUG (Laffranchi, 2001; Lourenço, 2003).

According to Lourenço (2003), during the 6th World Championship in Rotterdam in 1973, Brazil participated for the first time in the group competition, with a team coached by Ilona Peuker and finished in thirteenth place. Previous members of the GUG formed the first master group of gymnastics, called the Ilona Peuker Group and performed demonstrations in several regions of the country. According to Bernardes (2010):

> "All generations of successful coaches and gymnasts can consider themselves direct descendants of the work of Professor Ilona Peuker in Brazilian Rhythmic Gymnastics" (Bernardes, 2010, p. 56).

In Brazil there is great motivation for group competitions, the results of the Brazilian national team particularly the titles in the Pan-

American Games at Winnipeg (1999), Santo Domingo (2003), Rio de Janeiro (2007) and Guadalajara (2011) collaborated to increase club investments in all groups from the base to the adult category. Proof of this evolvement is the large number of teams in the Brazilian group championships, which takes place once a year, organized by the Brazilian Gymnastic Confederation (CBG), who renamed the event "Ilona Peuker" in 1998.

In Brazil, groups participate in all categories in Brazilian championships and national competitions. The state federations, 24 affiliated to the CBG today, also systematically promote group competitions at school level, initiation and high level in many age groups. Taking into consideration the results achieved by the Brazilian national team group, Nakajima and Reis (2006) believe that today, the technical level shown by the gymnasts in national competitions is perceptibly superior to previous performances. The Brazilian teams have created a personal culture of training, in this way achieving a more adequate base for the new challenges that arise in this discipline, bearing in mind that it is constantly changing with higher expectations every time.

The group competitions are the focus of our study, particularly the choreographic compositions which are organized according to specific rules of the technical regulations, governed by the International Gymnastic Federation. The national federations follow the rules of the rhythmic gymnastics' Code of Points edited by the FIG at each Olympic cycle. The typical characteristic of the group, formed by five gymnasts, is the participation of each member simultaneously in a homogeneous manner with a collective spirit. The composition must be conceived in a way that the idea of collaboration of all gymnasts at every point in the execution is clearly visible.

The different elements that collaborate in the creation of rhythmic gymnastics have given the sport an innovative character, expressionistic, clearly artistic, always noted in the movement of the gymnasts that, together with the correct musical accompaniment, promotes a harmonic relationship between body and equipment movements (Barbosa-Rinaldi, Martinelli, & Teixeira, 2009). Bueno (2010) argues that the group competition is a separate spectacle in rhythmic gymnastics. The symmetry, synchronism and expression of gymnasts combine to provide a show for spectators from around the world. Independent of category the composition and execution engage everyone.

The beauty of rhythmic gymnastics is translated through precise and creative movements that demonstrate the intention of the choreographer who, most of the time, is the coach. The group is capable of demonstrating all this choreographic value, in addition to the technical demands, within the maximum time of two minutes and thirty seconds through the subjective expressions of its gymnasts' performances which could be called a "choreographic event", making total transcendence possible for the watching spectators. (Lourenço, 2003; Lourenço & Gaio, 2010; Vidal, 1997):

> "To excel at Rhythmic Gymnastics is to reach the highest level of technical and artistic yield, and it is through this technical and artistic level that the coach realizes the recognition of her work, either from the public applause, or more obviously from the judges' grades, who score using a pre-established rule code, the objectivity and subjectivity of the composition. This subjectivity promotes differentiated evaluations, because each judge brings their own life experiences and, necessarily, faces the exhibition in different ways. Thus, it is not always the champion group which is the most praised, because the vision of the public isn't the same of the judges who, absolutely, search for technical accuracy within the beauty of the movements and the choreography as a whole" (Lourenço & Gaio, 2010, p. 378).

The group exercises always prove a great attraction to the public in general, highlighting the beauty of the apparatus trajectory, associated with the gymnasts´ movement, and the unforeseen cosmetic effects that emerge from these junctions, suggesting emotion and aesthetical feeling (Monteiro, 2000).

According to Bobo and Palmeiro (1998), the group represents a "special" modality in a sport clearly marked by individualism. The group is like a society that works with organized internal rules, leadership, recognition of each member´s possibilities and limitations, the separation of tasks according to each individual capacity.

This symbiosis is visible in the perfect relationship between gymnasts, primarily in what is referred to as the exchange of apparatus, collaborations and also synchronized moves. Monteiro (2000) quotes that in group exercises, throwing and exchanging of apparatus allows a communication between the gymnasts, based on relationships, collaborations and the elaboration of the choreography. In the group, the apparatus constitutes the core of the union and the connection between the five parts of the team.

A group in rhythmic gymnastics has peculiar characteristics, especially in the difficulties related to the exchange of apparatus between the members of the group and the organization of the collective work which can be executed with identical moves by all the gymnasts or different moves that fit the elements of the collaboration with or without rotating the body. The variety of ways to use the space is evidenced by the different chosen formations to perform the exercise in the official area of 13x13 meters. The organization of the choreographic exigencies must be faced as a training strategy and be part of the tactical preparation of the group. According to Laffranchi (2001) the tactical preparation in Rhythmic Gymnastics is synonymous with choreography development, creation of original moves and also the intention to highlight the gymnast's qualities, with the purpose of the composition being better than the opponents.

The group rating is no different to the individual. It is divided into two categories *difficulty (D)* and *execution (E)*. It is independently rated by two distinct groups of judges. Four judges rate difficulty. The highest and lowest ratings are eliminated and the two middle scores are used to calculate the average score. The same is done for execution. This bench is sometimes composed of five judges, and in this case the average score is calculated using the three middle ratings. The final score is calculated by summing both the E and D partial grades to reach a maximum of 20 points.

The difficulty judges evaluate the body difficulties in three major groups: jumps, balances and pivotal elements, they also grade the exchange difficulties, dance step combinations, the dynamic elements with rotation and throws, and the collaboration elements between the gymnasts with or without rotation that must be fluent in the choreography.

The members of the arbitration board for execution rate the artistic and technical faults of the group. Among the artistic faults there are issues related to unity, expressivity and musicality, organization of group-work, variety of moves such as utilization of space, and the technical faults are all the execution mistakes during a group competition. All the specifications that guide judge's ratings discussed in this text can be found in the Code of Points of the 13th rhythmic gymnastics cycle, published by the FIG which regulates the discipline from 2013 to 2016.

2.2 Musical accompaniment

In creating a group choreography, the first step it to choose the music for the exercise. The music must follow the gymnast's physical and psychological characteristics, in order to obtain the desired unity. It's important for the music to have a defined and well-marked rhythm and the gymnast or the group must demonstrate this rhythm through moves during the composition. The structure and conclusion must be precise and clear, and the end of the execution of all the gymnasts must coordinate perfectly with the music's last chord:

> "The music is, without doubt the starting point of a rhythmic gymnastics composition, without this it is impossible to give life to the discipline's specific movements and impossible to unify one element with another. The music is always associated with an image that guides the idea for the movements, their intonation and dynamic variations suggesting the utilization of a static element such as a balance, or an explosive movement like a jump, or perhaps nuances of undulation and soft movements" (Lourenço, 2003, p. 97).

To start and finish at the same time as the music isn't enough, all the choreography must be tied to the rhythm of the chosen song, in other words, the contrast of the moves in harmony with the time, rhythm and accents of the music must be respected, running the risk that if this doesn't happen then the group will present a totally out of context composition, commonly called "background music". Having the song as an initial inspiration for an RG composition, the set-up of the choreography can develop through and guide the idea like telling a story with technical, aesthetical and emotional elements, thereby the spectators can emotionally involve themselves with the presentation (Laffranchi, 2001; Lourenço, 2010).

In the current cycle, the music is extremely important principally with the requirement of eight second long dance steps and the novelty is the utilization of words in some choreographies used by groups, which was forbidden until 2012. This new rule, at first provisional, enables the creation of choreographic moves from the lyrics and not only from the musical arrangement, although this can be tricky if the content of the lyrics is not suitable for the age of the gymnasts or even for the sport choreography.

The interest in rescuing the triad of gymnast / music / apparatus can be clearly seen with the advent of more choreography which expresses the discipline's central concept of the union of these components in a harmonious way orchestrated by the chosen music for the exercise, harmony that has been lost in recent cycles which overstated the value of points and level of difficulty as the base for compositions.

The choice of music in alliance with the gymnast's expressions through body work, connected to the handling of the apparatus is the factor that gives stability between the choreography and group. The elaboration of the arrangements or music mixing must be done well. Napias (1997) found in a study during the World Championships in Paris a large number of songs with problems in the arrangement mounting that produced inconsistencies in musical plays. This problem is still found in current events.

Robeva (1997) affirms that the gymnast and choreographer are required to master certain knowledge such as timing, values and musical phrases, not mistaking dynamics with timing, in order not to run the risk of starting a new move in the middle of a musical phrase, this is certainly excellent advice corresponding to the current rules.

2.3 Difficulty

A group exercise must contain ten difficulties of which five are exchange and the other five are body elements. Exchanges are considered to be the performance of two actions: each gymnast throws their apparatus and retrieves one from another athlete. According to Lourenço (2010):

> *"Only exchanges performed by all the gymnasts and with throws (apparatus in the air) are validated. The exchanges can be of the same kind and level for all the gymnasts, or of different kinds and levels"* (Lourenço, 2010, p. 124).

The exchanges can be executed simultaneously or in quick succession and also with the gymnasts standing still or moving. Body difficulties are not allowed in exchange compositions, only body elements must be used added to all kinds of throws and recoveries of the apparatus in question, for example: throwing without using hands or out of the visual field, recovering the apparatus from the floor or maintaining a six-meter distance between the teammates. There is a table of options provided in the FIG Code of Points (2013/2016).

The maths is simple, to each new criterion a value of 0.10 points is added, and at least one criterion is required as base value. The groups must present their outlines prior to the competition so that the difficulty judges can evaluate them. Below is an example of a transcription of the competition spreadsheets, based on the requirements of the FIG 13th evaluation cycle. The letter E refers to exchange; 0.30 is the final value of this exchange; 0.10 for throwing in a body movement element (EC); 0.10 for the distance between the gymnasts in the moment of the execution (6 meters) and 0.10 for the apparatus recovery on the floor by all the gymnasts (RC, see Figure 2.1).

In compliance with the aforementioned code, to validate an exchange difficulty the apparatus should not fall, even one of the maces. In the case of the apparatus being dropped, the difficulty referees will

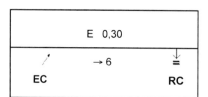

Figure 2.1: Symbology for exchanges.

not validate the exchange and yet points will be removed by the execution judges.

The body difficulties without exchange follow the same rule values as seen for the individual category, which range from 0.10 to 0.50 points. The three body groups must be mandatorily present and there is the possibility of increasing the grade by putting together jump, balance and rotation difficulties, additional rotation and wave criterions, although the mixed and multiple difficulties are not allowed in group choreographies, except fouetté. In research by Stahlschmidt (2012) on the 2011 Brazilian Group Championship, jump difficulties are the most common in infant, junior and senior category choreographies, with the pivot being the less utilized according to another segment of the research done by Pilati (2012), remembering that in the previous cycle, balance between the body difficulties wasn't necessary.

Lourenço, Bernardi and Colares (2012) carried out a study on exchanges in the same event and concluded that all the teams showed a minimal number of mandatory exchanges, however were very similar in the execution form. The most commonly presented body element criterion was the six meter distance and floor recuperation, a fact that should not occur in the current cycle as criterion repetitions are not allowed, inducing the coach to utilize, in the choreography, a great variety of launches and floor recuperations in the exchanges. A curiosity in this study is that even when it was possible to execute body difficulties during the exchange in the cycle, the teams opted not to include them and, even when they were included, only in the launches and not in the catches.

Dance is one of the factors that influenced rhythmic gymnastics during the emergence process of the discipline. The dance steps combinations presented in the current Code of Points replaced the rhythmic steps in the last code, however with bigger rhythmic intensity. Each choreography must contain at least one folk, modern, ballroom or other style of dance step sequence transmitting the character and emotions of the song. Dance step combinations can be very important allies to the team work organization because they can be performed in an identical form with or without displacement of the five gymnasts simultaneously or even in subgroups.

2.4 Relationship and collaboration between the gymnasts

According to the FIG Code of Points (2013/2016), "The typical character of the Group Exercise is the participation of each gymnast in the homogeneous work of the group in a spirit of cooperation" (p. 32), and it is the form of organization of this group work that will enable this exigency fluently to happen. When all the gymnasts execute the same kind of movement we can find organization with synchronized execution, in fast succession, in canon and contrast. When gymnasts execute different moves, we find the organization of the execution in coral and collaboration. The definitions of group organization aren't included in the Code of Points texts, so a better comprehension is found in Abruzzini's (1997) study:

- Synchronized execution: all movements are performed simultaneously with the same pace and intensity.

- Execution in rapid succession: each gymnast or subgroup performs the movement with a time delay relative to the other gymnast or subgroup and so forth.

- Execution in canon: usually used for a small combination of movements, the beginning of each member of the group or subgroup happens one or more times after.

- Execution in "contrast": of vitality (fast-slow), intensity (strong-weak), direction (front-rear) and level (high-low).

- Organization with execution in coral: each member of the group or subgroup performs their movement independent of the others, with the aim of a united result.

- Organization in collaboration with execution: each member of the group or subgroup makes a move in collaboration with their partner, with the aim of a common result.

For Lourenço (2003, p. 135), "it is important to emphasize that all these organizations within a specific composition of RG, must comply with the specific characteristics of the sport, namely the handling of the device and esthetics of gymnastics".

Passive actions continue to be considered as forbidden elements in rhythmic gymnastics compositions, these elements are easily identified such as when one or more gymnasts don't make their own moves but are carried or dragged by their teammates for more than two steps, walk with more than one support per gymnast or form pyramids (Lourenço, 2010). However, there is the possibility of letting creativity flow on gymnast's elevations which are often utilized in collaborations.

In the organization of group work, the collaboration elements are found when the gymnasts perform different moves, performed with or without body rotation. Collaboration without body rotation are those moves where all gymnasts participate and are in contact with one another if only by means of a device with the objective of a choreographic final result where the role of one depends on another. The gymnasts can be united or in subgroups, displaced or not in different ways and directions, launching or not including two or more apparatus simultaneously or successively by the same gymnast.

The principal characteristics of collaborations with body rotation is the loss of visual contact with the device that happens by executing a body rotation, in any direction, during the flight of the apparatus, and possibly passing over, under or through a teammate or the apparatus itself which can be secured by another gymnast or in the air. These collaborations are worth a higher score and are the most used in compositions.

According to research carried out by Santos (2012) and Araújo (2012) during the 2012 Brazilian Group Competition, 40% of collaborations in the choreographies displayed in infant, junior and senior categories were made without launches and the most common collaborations were those that required launches with loss of visual contact. An important detail is that generally only one of the gymnasts performed the action of passing over, under or through the gymnast/apparatus which leads us to think that one option of the coach was to not be too daring on collaborations in order to avoid losing execution notes:

> "The collaborations with throws, risk and loss of visual contact with the apparatus during its flight [...] totalled 36% of the total found in all choreographies. Although it isn't a very easy exercise to execute, it was well represented in the infant category choreographies, because of the seven analyzed teams, six presented at least three collaborations at this level and only one utilized this element just once. However it is important to point out that of the six groups that presented several elements at this level, only one of them did not commit any execution mistakes; the other teams did not receive 100% accuracy on the realization of risky collaborations" (Santos, 2012, p. 23).

Yet according to a study by Santos (2012) and Araújo (2012), the collaborations involving big throws of two or more apparatus simultaneously by one gymnast equalled 15% of the total of collaborations found in the research. The values for this kind of collaboration appeared in the 2009/2012 cycle, even though the teams had already shown these kinds of moves in past cycles, only in 2009 did the FIG RG technical committee decide to give a specific score to it. Considered at first to be a difficult execution, these moves became part of everyday life in groups including infant choreographies. In the case of this research six out of seven participating teams in this category performed this kind of collaboration.

2.5 Variety

The choice of body and apparatus elements must be varied and contemplate the maximum number of possible opportunities. The variety in the choice of elements is related to small and large, symmetrical and asymmetrical in different types, directions, planes, levels, shapes and dynamic movements.

Utilization of the space is also a demand in group compositions. The complete 13x13 meter area must be utilized during a choreography in a way that includes different directions (forwards, backwards, right and left), different trajectories (straight lines and sinuous curves), different planes (front, back, horizontal, and sagittal), different height levels (high, medium and low) and even different modalities (Barbosa-Rinaldi et al., 2009; FIG, 2013-2016; Lourenço, 2010):

> *"In relation to the types or modes, as they are called in the specific literature, these are defined as the way in which the offset or body element will be performed, such as waltz steps, hops, jumps, rhythmic steps, walkovers, forward, and movements supported by other parts of the body than the feet" (Lourenço, 2010, p. 132).*

Formations are the designs of the displacements in the competition area and a good choreographic composition must show formation variety, mainly with regard to extent. According to Lourenço (2010) formations can be observed from the different positions of the gymnasts on the competition platform during the execution of the choreography. Each group exercise should contain at least six different formations, with diverse amplitude (closed and open formations) and different directions. The composition of the group must use the entire surface of the floor. The training should be organized by the five gymnasts simultaneously or in different subgroups with different possibilities of division, creating formations themselves in each team. Gymnasts must not remain in the same formation for long.

The formation change occurs through the displacement of one or more members of the group, which means that only with a new positioning of one of the gymnasts is it possible to obtain a new line. These formations can be fixed with the gymnasts in their places, for example, performing a body difficulty or can be seen in movement. An example of formation in movement would be performing a series of hops or jumps or even a sequence of dance steps in a circle. Nothing prevents formations in subgroups, where one of the group is doing a static element and the other a dynamic displacement element. To Berra (1997) the formations in displacements are particularly used to better visualize jump difficulties.

During the World Championships of rhythmic gymnastics held in Paris in 1994, studies were performed on the different formations of group choreography. Berra (1997) identified 18 different types of formations, and formations in straight lines and triangles were the most used. He also found that over 50% of the teams participating in the competition used circle formations.

It is worth remembering that, at that time, the groups consisted of six titular gymnasts, which made formation easy in pairs and trios, characterizing drawings in the competition area that can't be executed in five-gymnast groups. The average number of formations encountered by Berra (1997) was nine for choreographies with only one apparatus and ten for choreographies with two distinct kinds of apparatus. Another fact that must be taken into account is that the groups could use longer than two minutes and thirty seconds.

Nowadays it is hard to find choreographic compositions that include few formations, actually we observe many designs during the exercise execution that are mainly dynamic, even though it is common to see the repetition of formations in the same choreography, which is not interesting.

Chagas (2012) analyzed 41 infant, junior and senior category choreographies during the Brazilian Group Championships in 2011 and the average was 20.2 formations, being in the majority (82%) open formations and the index of repetitions was very high, reaching 24% on the exercises with the tape in the senior category (Lourenço & Chagas, 2012).

Laffranchi (2001) presents a formations classification indicating a wide range of a total of 27 different formation possibilities for groups of five gymnasts with alignment positions of horizontal, vertical, diagonal or mixed and matched. We add here the circle or curvilinear formations that add more possibilities of organizing the space. Chagas (2012) also observed a scarce number of circle formations, only 8% of the formations found in analyzed choreographies at the Brazilian Group Championship in 2011 were of this kind, independent of the category. The circle-shaped or semi-circle formation aids the dynamism of the choreography and diversity of space occupation.

2.6 Final remarks

Once a choreographic composition is finished, the coach's task is arduous, starting a never-ending work of cleaning of moves that require countless repetitions. The expectation is an execution with no failures, ensuring that all the creative composition is visually perfect, in an extremely synchronized way even whilst knowing that 'perfection' doesn't exist.

There are a lot of details to think about in a group composition, all the rules and considerations detailed here are a basis for the reflections of the professionals, which will enable a true choreographic event to happen, that can be admired by the public and perceived by all the people involved as the uniqueness of this sport, that requires more than ever, creative innovation in the choice of music and group work organization.

References

Abruzzini, E. (1997). L' exercice d'ansemble em grs: la corégraphie. G.R.S. *Le sens d'une evolution, 18/19*, 11-19.

Araújo, L. (2012). *Análise das Dificuldades de Colaboração nas Coreografias de Conjunto: categoria Juvenil - campeonato brasileiro de conjuntos de ginástica rítmica "Ilona Peuker" / 2011. 2012, 34f.* (Monografia especialização em ginástica rítmica). Universidade Norte do Paraná, Londrina.

Barbosa-Rinaldi, I. P., Martinelli, T. A. P., & Teixeira, R. S. (2009). *Ginástica Rítmica: história, características, elementos corporais e música*. Maringá, PR: Eduem.

Bernardes, G. (2010). Revivendo o meu encontro com a ginástica rítmica. In E. Paolielo, & E. de Toledo (Eds.), *Possibilidades da ginástica rítmica* (pp. 45-71). São Paulo: Phorte Editora.

Berra, M. (1997). Analyse de quelques constantes des compositions d'esembles. G.R.S. *Le sens d'une evolution, 18/19*, 75-81.

Bobo, M., & Palmeiro, M. A (1998). *Ximnasia Rítmica Deportiva - adestramento e competición*. Santiago de Compostela: Edicións Lea.

Bueno, T. F. (2010). Ginástica Rítmica exercício de conjunto: cinco ginastas, um só corpo. In E. Paolielo, & E. de Toledo (Eds.), *Possibilidades da ginástica rítmica* (pp. 218-236). São Paulo: Phorte Editora.

Chagas, F. H. (2012). *Análise das formações em coreografias de conjunto: uma visão geral do campeonato brasileiro de conjuntos de ginástica rítmica "Ilona Peuker"/2011. 2012, 47f.* (Monografia especialização em ginástica rítmica). Universidade Norte do Paraná, Londrina.

Fédération Internationale de Gymnastique (FIG) (2013-2016). *Code of points rhythmic gymnastics*. Technical Committee rhythmic gymnastics.

Laffranchi, B. (2001). *Treinamento desportivo aplicado à ginástica rítmica*. Londrina: UNOPAR.

Lourenço, M. R. A. (2003). *Ginástica rítmica no Brasil: a (r)evolução de um esporte*. (Master's thesis). Universidade Metodista de Piracicaba, Piracicaba.

Lourenço, M. R. A. (2010). O inconstante código de pontuação da ginástica rítmica. In E. Paolielo, & E. de Toledo (Eds.), *Possibilidades da ginástica rítmica* (pp. 111-140). São Paulo: Phorte Editora.

Lourenço, M. R. A., & Gaio, R. (2010). Ginástica rítmica: reflexões sobre arte e cultura. In R. Gaio, A. A. Gois, & J. C. F. Batista (Eds.), *A ginástica em questão: corpo e movimento* (2nd ed., pp. 361-380). São Paulo: Phorte Editora.

Lourenço, M. R. A., Bernardi, L. M. de O., & Colares, A. K. de S. (2012). Análise das dificuldades de troca nas coreografias de conjunto: categoria juvenil – Campeonato Brasileiro de Conjuntos de Ginástica Rítmica de 2011. In L. M. Schiavon, E. Toledo, M. A. C. Bortoleto, & M. Nunomura (Eds.), *III Seminário Internacional de Ginástica Artística e Rítmica de Competição* (pp. 35-43). Rio Claro: Biociências de Rio Claro.

Lourenço, M. R. A., & Chagas, F. H. (2012). Análise das formações nos conjuntos da categoria adulto participantes do campeonato brasileiro de ginástica rítmica de 2011. In L. M. Schiavon, E. Toledo, M. A. C. Bortoleto, & M. Nunomura (Eds.), *III Seminário Internacional de Ginástica Artística e Rítmica de Competição* (pp. 44-52). Rio Claro: Biociências de Rio Claro.

Monteiro, S. G. P. (2000) *Quantificação e classificação das cargas de treino em ginástica rítmica: Estudo de caso – Preparação para o campeonato do mundo de Osaka 1999 da seleção nacional e conjuntos senior.* (Master's thesis). Faculdades de Ciências do Desporto de Educação Física da Universidade do Porto.

Nakashima, F. S., & Reis, L. N. (2006). *Treinamento em ginástica rítmica no estado do Paraná.* (Monografia especialização em ginástica rítmica). Universidade Norte do Paraná, Londrina.

Napias, F. (1997). Analyse descriptive dês montages et arrangementes musicaux dans lês exercises individuels. *Le sens d'une evolution, 18/19*, 91-99.

Pilati, S. A. C. (2012). *Análise das dificuldades de salto nas coreografias de conjunto: uma visão geral das coreografias do campeonato brasileiro de conjuntos de ginástica rítmica de 2011.* (Monografia especialização em ginástica rítmica). Universidade Norte do Paraná, Londrina.

Robeva, N. (1997) Composition des exercises individuals. *Le sens d'une evolution, 18/19*, 47-58.

Santos, E. V. N. dos, Lourenço, M. R. A., & Gaio, R. (2010). *Composição coreográfica em ginástica rítmica: do compreender ao fazer.* Jundiaí: Fontoura.

Santos, P. F. dos. (2012). *Análise das colaborações em coreografias de conjunto: uma visão geral das categorias infantil e adulto do campeonato brasileiro de conjuntos de ginástica rítmica "Ilona Peuker" / 2011.* (Monografia especialização em ginástica rítmica). Universidade Norte do Paraná, Londrina.

Stahlschmidt, K. (2012). *Análise das dificuldades de pivot nas coreografias de conjunto: campeonato brasileiro de conjunto de ginástica rítmica de 2011.* (Monografia especialização em ginástica rítmica). Universidade Norte do Paraná, Londrina.

Vidal, A. M. (1997). *La dimensión artística de la gimnasia rítmica deportiva. Análisis del conjunto como acontecimiento coreográfico.* Galícia: Centro Galego de Documentación e edicións Deportivas.

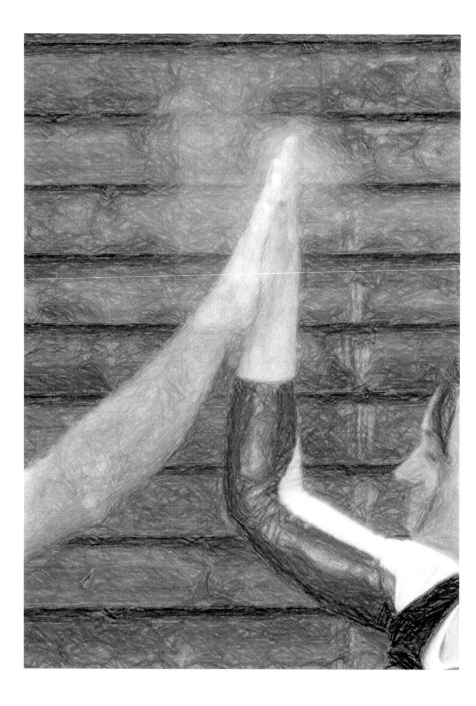

CHAPTER 3

PROFILE, MOTIVATIONS AND THE CHALLENGES OF ARTISTIC GYMNASTICS COACHES IN BRAZIL

Myrian Nunomura[1] & Mauricio Santos Oliveira[1,2]

[1] *University of São Paulo - School of Physical Education and Sport (Brazil).*
Correspondence to: mnunomur@usp.br

[2] *Federal University of Espírito Santo - Physical Education and Sports Center (Brazil).*
Correspondence to: mauoliveira@usp.br

Acknowledgement:
The content of this chapter is based on the research "Diagnosis of Sport Development Process in Artistic Gymnastics in Brazil" and it was supported by São Paulo Research Foundation (FAPESP).

3.1 Introduction

When we contemplate the performance of the Brazilian gymnasts Daiane dos Santos and Arthur Zanetti, we can attribute their success in artistic gymnastics (AG) to their talent, efforts, dedication, originality, technique mastery, and to the high difficulty skills that they present. However, their potential to sport would not be accomplished without the targeting and follow up of a competent and dedicated coach.

The gymnasts are heavily dependent on the coaches, in a significant way, who through their experience, knowledge and dedication play a determinant role in the athletes' development. The great coach Boris Pilkin from Russia used to say that, in AG context, "coaches can be likened to roots; you see the flowers, not the roots" (Langsley, 2000, p. 66).

Therefore, we can infer that the gymnasts are spotlighted in the AG, but the backstage working of the coaches is essential to offer subsidies and support the process of development and the achievement of their athletes' results. The gymnasts grow, develop and flourish with the objective of displaying their qualities to the world, while coaches nourish their talent and provide support for their athletes.

Being an AG coach is a job that involves dilemmas and difficult decisions, which turns it into a challenging profession. Besides planning and implementing actions, which may favor the technical, tactical, physical and artistic development of the gymnasts, coaching also involves psychological and situational aspects. Moreover we must emphasize that each gymnast is a unique individual, who will demand a specific skill of the coach and, therefore, it will make coaching even complex.

Profile, motivations, and the challenges of AG coaches. 43

The context of the AG coaches' intervention generates different challenges to this profession, which are not limited to pedagogical, attitudinal or intellectual issues. We also must relate the physical and psychological burden that falls on coaches in the course of their coaching in and outside the gym.

Coaches deal with demands of gymnasts, parents, clubs, media, and of the coaches themselves. Another factor, not less important, includes the work condition, which influences on the coaches' daily coaching. Motivated by these issues, the present chapter aims to present and discuss the AG coaches' profile in Brazil, their work conditions, their motivation to coach in this sport and the challenges presented in their daily coaching in the gyms, which develop the gymnasts in Brazil.

3.2 Methodological procedures

In order to identify, analyze and discuss the profiles, motivation, and challenges of AG coaches in Brazil, we have interviewed 46 AG coaches, who are coaching in 29 different institutions in Brazil. Thirty four coaches are coaching women and 12 coaches are coaching men.

To select the coaches, we contacted the State Federations aiming to identify the affiliated institutions which keep regular participation in the official tournaments in the following categories: pre-infant (9-10 years), infant (10-12 years), infant-juvenile (12-14 years), and juvenile (14-18 years) in the men's AG. The categories in the women's AG were: pre-infant (9-10 years), infant (10-12 years), and juvenile (12-15 years).

The scope of the study was restricted to the state of São Paulo and the cities of Rio de Janeiro, Curitiba and Porto Alegre due to the representativeness of these places in the national competitive scenario of this sport. In order to organize the data, the coaches are indicated with the abbreviation C (coach) followed by a numbering. The institutions that had more than one coach got, besides the abbreviation C, a classificatory letter was used, for example, C10A.

For data treatment, we have used content analysis (Bardin, 2008) as a technique to organize and reduce the obtained information in the field in order to make inferences. We highlight that we did not have any interest regarding the quantitative analysis of the coaches' statements, but to discourse about the latent contents of the messages.

The study has been submitted and approved by the ethics committee in research from the School of Physical Education and Sport at the University of São Paulo.

3.3 The profile of artistics gymnastics coaches in Brazil

It is crucial to know AG coaches' profile, to be able to understand their actions in the coaching process. Authors, such as Mallett and Côté (2006) cite that, in the high performance sport, coaches are greatly held liable for results in the competition, although they are not able to control all the factors that could influence in a champion's determination, for example, an acute injury.

The success of AG depends on the proper planning, organization, administration, execution and evaluation of the coaching process, for only this way, the gymnast will reach the desired progress and will accomplish his/her top potential (Arkaev & Suchilin, 2004; Readhead, 1993; Smoleuskiy & Gaverdouskiy, 1996). This aspect is meaningfully related to the coach's skills in different fields of knowledge, such as anatomy, physiology, biomechanics, pedagogy, nutrition, sporting management, and psychology. Therefore we have confirmed the need for qualified professionals, who can meet the different demands of this sport.

Nunomura (2004) mentions that there are specific international educational programs for professionals who wish to coach AG, and that they are developed in an integrated system between associations and federations. In Brazil the situation is distinct, as there is no educational system for the development of professionals, who aim to follow a coach career. The establishing of associations is not a part of our culture yet, and neither the State Federations nor the National Confederation has created a system for the education and qualification of gymnastic coaches. So, this responsibility is in charge of the higher education.

We have observed that, among the 46 coaches that were interviewed in the study, 44 are graduated in physical education. Certainly, there is a relation between this fact and the current requirements for this profession. Since the regulation of the physical education as a profession (Law 9696/1998; Brazil, 1998), to play the coach role, it became necessary the registration at the board, which supervises this profession, and it requires a higher education.

We verified that only two coaches did not have accomplished academic education, however one coach was attending the physical education course at the time of the interview, while the other one did not have any academic education.

After consulting 41 physical education courses in Brazil, the study of Nunomura (2001) evidenced that 35 of them offered the AG subject in their curriculum, and seven of them offered advanced studies in AG with the objective of deepening the theoretical and empirical knowledge in this sport. The author has concluded, after consulting the summary of these subjects, that such disciplines are offered with an emphasis in the fundamentals of this sport, aiming above all, to be eligible to coach at the initiate level of AG. Therefore it did not offer enough subsidies for the education of coaches, who intend to coach AG at the highest level.

Due to the above-mentioned reasons, 20 coaches invested in their post-graduation and got the title of expert, specialization (lato senso), what represents an effort to be better qualified, particularly, trying to acquire the necessary knowledge to answer the demand of the high performance sport.

We must highlight that many coaches also fall back upon short term courses that offer subsidies for their coaching, mainly because this sport is in a continuous process of evolution, caused by the dynamic of the Code of Points and the development of new skills and teaching methods.

We have identified that the average time of coaching was of 12.85 years, what reveals a reasonable experience in the competitive sector. By and large, the coaches with long experience and coaching time are nominated for the role of AG coordinator, in their respective worksites.

At the moment of the study, the length of time that the coaches were working at the current institution varied among 10 months to 20 years, an average of 8.73 years. Supported in these data, we believe that there is a certain professional stability, mainly, at the public sector as the admission is done through a tendering process and the permanent characteristic of the public jobs in Brazil.

The diversity of intervening factors in the coaching process, requires the support of a multidisciplinary team (FIG, 2003), but in the Brazilian context the majority of the coaches cannot count on the support of professionals from other fields, what increases their responsibilities and tasks.

Along the interviews, we found that just few number of coaches have assistants or a multidisciplinary team to assist them at work that demands the knowledge, skills and qualification in other fields beyond the AG itself. Many coaches mentioned that they miss the support from psychologist and nutritionist in the process of training.

Besides coaching without support from assistants or from a multidisciplinary team, we confirmed that the number of athletes that are under the responsibility of only one coach is high, when considering the need of attention that the competitive sector requires, and the specificity of the training, which most of the time is individualized. Another aggravating factor is the need, of most of the coaches, to work simultaneously with different categories. The particular nature of the teaching process of this sport requires physical assistance (spotting), regular feedback, guidance, among other pedagogical actions that demand, exceptionally, the coach's presence (Nunomura, 1998, 2005).

Another issue which came out during the study, concerns to the low number of coaches who have a contact or a partnership with the scholars. Nevertheless, some of the coaches mentioned the importance of studies, which could support their work. Two problems were evident: the coach, who does not seek for the university because of lack of time, and the scholars that have not been searching for partnerships with coaches and training centers.

In contrast with some of the challenges faced in the AG coaches' education in our country, we highlight that the coaches of the formative categories in Brazil, who foster the national team, have developed a very effective job. It is noticeable that most of them were able to develop promising gymnasts getting significant results nationally and internationally.

3.4 Motivations for the coaches to coach artistic gymnastics

It is important to understand the reasons that motivated the coaches to coach AG. From their identification, we could take actions that would enhance the number of coaches in the field (Winterstein, 1992).

The theoretical grounding of our study is the motivation related to the interactional model between the individual and the situation. According to Weinberg and Gould (2001), this model considers that the sport motivation depends on personal factors, those related to individual characteristics, as much as on factors related to situations and conditions around the individual. Therein, motivation can be understood according to its origin, i.e., intrinsic or extrinsic. Lopes (2009) as well Massimo and Massimo (2013) associate the intrinsic motivation to personal factors related to feelings, and that they do not have any relation to external elements. Consequently, the extrinsic motivation is related to the environmental factors, to the influences of others and to the external rewards, as the recognition.

We highlight that both ways influence mutually through the extrinsic and intrinsic mechanism of reinforcement (Samulski, 1992). Carron, Hausenblas and Estabrooks (2003) indicate that the kind of motivation expressed by the individual will impact on his/her choices, dedication, persistence, and in the passion concerning the activities. Therefore, we set our interest in understanding the reasons which motivate the high performance coaches to coach.

(1) Previous experience in artistic gymnastics

A significant number of coaches have been motivated by their previous experience in AG when choosing their current profession. The insertion in this sport context happened mostly when they still were athletes, as we can observe in the following reports: "I was a gymnast and I trained for many years, it was a passion" (C12). "I was an athlete, so I enjoyed it, I identified myself and liked it a lot" (C17). "I was gymnast, I can't foresee my life without it. It gets into your blood, and won't go out anymore" (C29A).

Oliveira (2010) reports that the number of former gymnasts, who coach in Brazil is large. However, the author highlights that we have to make a critic reflection about this fact, because only the experience as an athlete does not guarantee the success as a coach. According to Nista-Piccolo (2003):

> *"A former athlete will always have the advantage of having lived some moments that are very close to those that his/her team will experience. Understanding the taste of victories as well as the defeats, the path becomes more pleasant, but it does not guarantee the success, and not even will make us sure that the work has been well done" (Nista-Piccolo, 2003, p. 11).*

Some coaches mentioned their experience as an AG assistant before accomplishing their physical education course: "When I practiced, I helped my instructor, and as time went by I continued there" (C10). "I was gymnast and I trained in the morning, and an assistant in the afternoon" (C29C). "I started practicing gymnastics and...I don't know, it went on and I started helping, and here I am up to now" (C21).

This previous relation with AG runs in the results of Nunomura (2001), when the author tackled the professional formation in this sport. The author states that many coaches rely their coaching methods, on their experience as an athlete and/or in their athletic prestige due to the titles conquered during their career. This fact seems to be usual in sport in general, and we can observe the eloquent presence of former athletes in the sport system as coaches, leaders, or referees.

On the other hand, we notice a certain dissatisfaction of some coaches, even saying they enjoyed the sport, and a more surprising one, who emphasized that "unfortunately" he made that professional option: "If it was for me to choose it today, I wouldn't. I think it is ungrateful. You work a lot for no results. The satisfaction you get is very little. You just work to survive, there is no reward, you don't even get respect as a coach... there is no support, who is more valued? Who develop the athlete or the one who get him prepared to compete at the high level of sport?" (C2).

The recognition of ones work is considered paramount to the adherence of the coaches (Inglis, Danylchuk, & Pastore, 1996). When the coach does not perceive the recognition of his/her work, as through financial incentive or prestige and support, the lack of this aspect turns into a source of stress (Olusoga et al., 2009), and it becomes a reason to dropout the profession (Gould et al., 1990).

Although C2 presents significant results in the AG context, the coach has a problematical attitude towards the sport when coaching children and youth, considering the influence the coach has as a model in the development of youth's personality (Campbell, 1998; Haines, 1989). The reflection of C2's negative view can directly fall upon the sporting life of their gymnasts, and also upon their professional choice, because they may be dissuaded to coach AG.

Although there is a great number of coaches with former experience in AG, the data revealed that the coaches' athletic experience in this sport is not a determinant factor to achieve success in the professional career at the highest level of sport, as many institutions, and the coaches themselves believe, and the fact reinforces the results of Nunomura (2001).

Some coaches reported that they do not have a former experience with AG, but, irrespective of this fact, they got significant results in the national scenario and, in some cases, in the international level. We cannot deny that the athlete's experience could contribute to the coaches' coaching. But, in opposition, it can also be unfavorable, if we consider that many of them can propagate their experiences, without a critical reflection over them, or even aim results which they did not accomplished in their sporting career, transferring this frustration and responsibility to their own athletes.

(2) Necessity of subsistence

The need of many young people to enter in the labor market as soon as possible, mainly to help the family subsistence, made the coaches C6 and C15 to start their professional career at AG: "I have never been an AG athlete, and I needed and I went" (C6). "I needed to work and ended up being interested about it" (C15). As for C6, in spite of never having been an athlete and not having a previous contact with this sport, he accepted the job opportunity to coach AG.

Some coaches that are former athletes said that to get a scholarship, they accepted the job in AG: "I wanted to study in a private school, so at the age of 14 I started as an assistant" (C10A). "I needed to pay college, they offered me the apprenticeship" (C25).

(3) Pleasure, fondness for the practice

According to Lyle, Allison and Taylor (1997), the feeling of pleasure being and acting as a coach is one of the main reasons that keep the coaches involved in the sport career. Moreover, it keeps up their interest and involvement in the competition and in the athletes' development.

This pleasure can be observed in the following statements: "I like to be a coach, it is a personal accomplishment" (C2). "Desire to be an instructor, to be a gymnastics coach" (C7). Some reports are rather emotional and demonstrate the fondness for AG, and that the positive experiences as gymnasts, led them to this professional choice: "I love AG, I have idealism... I have an objective in life, which is to coach athletes, to work with training" (C15). "It (AG) fulfills myself, it is really nice to have an objective, which is to work on what you enjoy. I didn't get to be an athlete, but AG got me" (C26). "I can't figure out my life without gymnastics" (C28). "We are very happy with what we do... it is a life choice for me ... I would do this all over again ... Gymnastics drove me to this happiness that I have as a professional... I got it through gymnastics... I am very happy working with gymnastics... I do it with love... gymnastics is in my heart" (C29A). This aspect leads us to believe that, if the experiences in sport are positive, there will be an impact on the former athletes' important decisions and among them in the professional career.

(4) Job opportunity
Although the coaches did not have any experience or a previous knowledge about the sport, some viewed in AG the possibility of a job through training, and also a professional position without a demand of previous experience, for those who were searching for the first job.

The anxiety in beginning a traineeship in the physical education field, led C29B to work with this sport: "I was a trainee at college and needed to work, needed to get anything, I wanted to work in this field" (C29B). Besides him, C15 also found in AG the possibility of

Profile, motivations, and the challenges of AG coaches. 53

working: "since the 1st year of college, it was the first job I got" (C15).

It does not seem very common to find high performance coaches, who do not have, at least, a brief experience as practitioners. Surprisingly, some of them have been distinguished in this role. Three coaches (C9, C15, C29B), who had been coaching the national team for a period of time at the centralized training center, did not have any contact with this sport, prior to coaching. Another coach (C15), who stands out in the male sector was a volleyball athlete. This coach linked his frustration as practitioner of another sport and the financial need to opt for the AG coach career.

We could mention the example of the coach Bela Karolyi, who coached the great Romanian gymnast Nadia Comaneci, and didn't have any practical experience in AG prior to his role as a coach. And, besides that, he was responsible for the success of many gymnasts who reached the Olympic and world podiums.

(5) External incentive

We stand out that this category aroused only among the women artistic gymnastics' coaches who reported that they opted for the coach career because they have been motivated by their teachers during college. It shows the impact of mentoring and the academic environment on the students future decisions: "I fell in love for the AG sport in college" (C27). "In college I started appreciating it (AG)" (C3). "I started having interest about it (AG) during college, while helping a teacher" (C14). "College was determinant. In the 1st semester we already had the AG subject, had the first contact with it, I was training a little more of acrobatics, mini-tramp… there was a gymnastic project, which gave the opportunity for everyone to work as an assistant" (C19).

The family influence also motivated one of the coaches to opt for this work. According to C23, his sister began coaching AG in the city where they lived, what motivated her decision to enter in the world of gymnastic. Such report is consistent with Harris (1999) who shows that some people take on certain day to day practices, if these are culturally transmitted, i.e., the tastes and the personalities of those who are responsible for them (parents), family and the social environment in which they live.

The opportunities offered by other people who coach AG, were also crucial for the coaches C11 and C14. In the first case, after having an injury during her athletic career, the coach decided to ask her to help in his work, encouraging her not to be only an athlete, but remain involved in AG, in another position. As for the second, her coach, who was responsible for the local team, motivated her to be a trainee in the gym.

Through these two reports, we can infer that the mentoring of their former coaches was crucial in some case to the decision to become an AG coach. We can relate it to the motivation felt by the young gymnasts when they can observe other athletes and work with experienced coaches.

Studies conducted by Lopes and Nunomura (2007) identified that 55% of the athletes in the high level of AG felt motivated by watching other athletes during trainings, competition and exhibition, and also that the coach's profile contributes to the motivation and adherence in the practice.

Bock, Furtado and Teixeira (2007) and Rúbio et al. (2000), mention the impact of the media on people's choices and decisions. The authors call attention to the influence of the high exposure of certain sports on TV, and athletes who are considered supermen, and that motivate the practice of sports by the public, in general.

The substantial increase in the international achievements of the Brazilian gymnasts, represented by medals in different stages of the World Cups, the Pan-American Games, and also the World Championships, served as a driving force for a wider dissemination of AG in the Brazilian media. And consequently, enable greater recognition of this sport and of their idols in the society (Carvalho, 2007).

Two coaches had the former gymnast Nadia Comaneci as inspiration for their current job: "the boom of Nadia that was going on TV motivated me a lot. I practiced with the adult group, I entered PE College and started it" (C24). "I have always enjoyed it... after watching Nadia, I fell in love" (C13).

In the context of Brazilian coaches, we could relate the Brazil Olympic award which has a great impact nationally and awarded the AG coaches Oleg Ostapenko and Renato Araújo, as the best coaches of the year in 2005 and 2009, respectively. This national recognition may arouse the interest of future professionals for this sport that presents an exponential progression in Brazil, in the beginning of the XXI century.

3.5 Daily challenges of the coaches

Nunomura and Nista-Piccolo (2003) report that, the lack of infrastructure influences the quality of coaching, mainly due to the need of high quality apparatus and equipments that could support the teaching and learning process of AG skills.

Dianno (1988) mentions that, when we watch an AG competition, we cannot figure out the difference that exists between training and infrastructure conditions among the participating teams in Brazil. In many gyms the apparatus are old and precarious, compromising the safety and health of gymnasts, besides disturbing the learning process. We were able to observe this fact through the coaches' statements: "the equipment is 15 years old and has never been remodeled, money is scarce" (C3). "the equipments are not good" (C16B). "our equipments need maintenance" (C11). "the equipment is obsolete" (C22B). "lack of equipment" (C22C).

According to Dianno (1988), several teams develop their AG programs in gyms that do not have the appropriate dimensions for this sport practice, a condition that also appeared in the coaches' words: "the room is very small, I would like to have a larger room" (C1). "our physical space is very small" (C28). "The space is shared with the trampoline, there is no room" (C20).

The difficulty in finding appropriate equipment for practicing, outruns with the lack of companies that manufacture them according to FIG specifications with affordable price for the teams. Oliveira and Bortoleto (2011) declare that, until now, any Brazilian company that produces AG equipment has the FIG homologation, and it is very likely that it occurs due to the little demand in the national market and also to the lack of necessary investments to manufacture the equipment according to specifications and technical patterns which are required by FIG. The authors believe that this condition may interfere in the development of AG in Brazil, as the national equipment does not match those international standards, which have safety and quality warranty.

The scarcity and quality problems of the equipment, and the size of the gyms do not only coincide with those teams with less national repercussion, but the top teams also face the same difficulty.

Oliveira (2010) declares that the athletes from the national team face the same problems, and just a few teams are able to obtain the equipment that are FIG approved, due to the high importation costs (prices and taxes).

Another challenge faced by AG coaches is related to the financial issue. The coaches mention the scarce financial resource for maintaining the team, the athletes and themselves: "money is scarce" (C3). "financial difficulties, always" (C22A). "the income isn't enough" (C22C).

Some individuals declare that the financial issue constrains the participation of athletes in competitive events, according to the following reports: "problems to go to the competition" (C9). "there isn't much support, the difficulty is taking them to compete out of the country, because in that case there isn't money" (C18). "there is a competition that we want to take part, and sometimes the cost is too high and they won't pay it" (C21). Each institution must bear the costs of a competition, which are not low. Oliveira (2010) mentions that the costs concerning the trip, accommodation, meals, and fees contribute to complicate even more the participation of a greater number of institutions in the national championships.

As we have observed in the reports, the financial issues make it difficult to participate in some desirable tournaments, mainly those organized by the Brazilian Gymnastics Confederation, which current politics is to encourage the AG practice in the states where this sport still does not have much popularity. However, many times, the states that don't have a gymnastics culture are far from the cities and states that have a greater number of teams and athletes. So, although this initiative has its merits, it is also important to consider the situation of the participating institutions, which actually have been trying hard to keep a regular participation in the national tournaments.

One of the coaches mentioned other problem related to athletes, who dropout when they reach the age to start working: "difficulty is when the girls are in an age to start working, and can't train anymore" (C13). Although this aspect has arisen in the women's category, it is more evident among male gymnasts, who reach their peak around 20 years of age, and for that reason, many of them leave the sport to complement their families' income.

Besides facing the dropout, coaches also mention the difficulties in attracting the children to this sport: "(problem) to get male athletes ... female we can find anywhere" (C2). "in the women's category, there was a larger flow of girls having classes than in the men's side. Difficulty to bring (boys), and then keep them" (C10). "it is hard when you don't have 'human resources' to work" (C5). According to the coaches', the difficulty in recruiting athletes to the men's AG is bigger, mainly due to the social and cultural aspects of this sport in the Brazilian society.

Concerning human resources, the coaches mention the lack of a multidisciplinary team and the scarcity of coaches and assistants, who could share the work in the gym: "hiring more teachers" (C23). "it is hard to keep a group of assistants" (C25). "there is no human resource, as a nutritionist, to give you support" (C22C).

Another challenge is related to the philosophy of the institution as it will influence the way the coach coaches their athletes: "it is the most political part, their decisions influence directly in our daily lives (at the gym), any big institution has its obstacles when dealing with many people, with different interests" (C17). The coaches mention that some institutions just worry about the number of gymnasts, without considering their development in the sport: "they only worry about the number of gymnasts inside the gym aiming to take them out of the streets, they don't want to see their sport progress, and that isn't our way of working" (C26). "the problem with the City Hall is the philosophy of whom is on the command ... So, he was worried about the number of students and to offer this sport to a great number of people" (C14).

In opposition, other institutions ask for competitive results: "the director asks if we were going to win, because otherwise we didn't need to travel (to the competition)" (C9). "if the team didn't get to be classified for the Open Games, the money, which is supposed to be paid in 10 installments, is blocked off" (C24). "it comes from the top, there is this charging that generates another one, and another, until it reaches the girls" (C29B). We noticed that, many times the coaches are demanded for results, even if they do not get proportional incentives to the pressures they suffer, and consequently it will have an impact on the young gymnasts.

3.6 Closing thoughts

As most of the Brazilian AG coaches have a degree in physical education, we suppose that all of them acquired the necessary knowledge that support their coaching and competencies to initiate gymnasts in their first steps in this sport.

It would be important and advisable that coaches seek for AG courses that will complement the knowledge they got at university, mostly, due to the limited time and few subjects in gymnastics offered at physical education courses. Other important aspect is related to the new methods and knowledge that are developed over the years. Therefore, updating is essential to improve him/herself as a coach.

However, we come to the following questions: Are there AG specialization courses or enough scientific groundings offered in higher education? Are there meetings nurturing the exchange of experiences among the professionals in Brazil?

We agree with Nunomura (2001), who proposes the creation of a Gymnastics Association in Brazil, in which the dialogue among the several institutions that are involved with this sport would be possible, especially universities, federations, and sports centers, aiming to promote the education, qualification and updating of professionals involved in AG.

Another important initiative involves scientific events, such as SIGARC (International Seminar of Competitive Artistic and Rhythmic Gymnastics). It has a great value in the coaches' education, due to the knowledge presented and discussed, especially, those related to the high level of sport. Moreover, this kind of event makes possible to coaches to join other professionals and academics, and share experiences.

During the study we realized that many coaches did not have a previous experience with this sport as a gymnast. We hope that this aspect will stimulate those professionals who feel apprehensive with the supposed disadvantage regarding the former gymnasts to get involved with the sport.

An additional highlighted role that the university could play in the AG specialized education, would be to offer opportunities for the undergraduate students to experience the teaching and learning process of AG in the extension programs at the university, which allows the practice of coaching in an actual learning process.

Our study also points out that the gymnastics lecturer at the higher education can be one of the greatest motivators for the coming coaches.

Then, it is essential that the faculty members are conscious of their disseminating and encouraging role in this sport.

Regarding coaches' work conditions, the study revealed that despite many of them do not have benefited from the satisfactory conditions of work (i.e. physical infrastructure, FIG approved apparatus, human resources and institutional support), it was still possible to observe outstanding results. The logic that explains the fact relies on devoted coaches and athletes who invest in their on careers. This situation allow them to keep the quality of their work and results, added to the support of local government and few sport clubs in Brazil.

This reality reveals that Brazil has a potential to stand out even more in the international sporting scenario, as there are both talented coaches and athletes. However, the efforts and investments should be shared among all those who are involved in the development of this sport in the country.

References

Arkaev, L., & Suchilin, N. (2004). *Gymnastics: how to create champions*. Oxford: Meyer & Meyer Sport.

Bardin, L. (2008). *Análise de conteúdo*. Lisboa: Edições 70.

Bock, A. M. B., Furtado, O., & Teixeira, M. L. T. (2007). *Psicologias: uma introdução ao estudo da psicologia*. São Paulo: Saraiva.

Brasil (1988). *Lei n. 9.696, de um de setembro de 1988*. Retrived from: http://www.planalto.gov.br/ccivil03/Leis/L9696.htm.

Campbell, S. (1998). A função do treinador no desenvolvimento do jovem atleta. *Revista Treino Desportivo, 1*(3), 31-36.

Carron, A., Hausenblas, H., & Estabrooks, P. (2003). *The Psychology of physical activity*. Boston: McGraw-Hill.

Carvalho, S. (2007). *O discurso midiático da ginástica artística*. (Master's thesis). Catholic University of Brasília, Brasília, Brazil.

Dianno, M. V. (1988). A ginástica olímpica no Brasil. *Revista Brasileira de Ciência e Movimento, 2*(2), 57-59.

Fédération Internationale de Gymnastique (FIG) (2003). *Age groups development program*. Montier: Fédération Internationale de Gymnastique.

Gould, D., Giannini, J., Krane, V., & Hodge, K. (1990). Educational needs of elite U.S. national team, pan american and olympic coaches. *Journal of Teaching in Physical Education, 9*(4), 332-344.

Haines, K. (1989). *Coaching certification manual*. Ontario: Gymnastics Canada Gymnastique.

Harris, J. R. (1999). *Diga-me com quem anda*. Rio de Janeiro: Editora Objetiva.

Inglis, S., Danylchuk, K. E., & Pastore, D. (1996). A conceptual framework for understanding retention factors in coaching and athletic management positions. *Journal of Sport Management, 10*(3), 237-249.

Langsley, E. (2000). *Gymnastics in perspective*. Mountier: Fédération Internationale de Gymnastique.

Lopes, P., & Nunomura, M. (2007) Motivação para a prática e permanência na Ginástica Artística de alto nível. *Revista Brasileira de Educação Física e Esporte, 21*(3), 177-187.

Lopes, P. (2009). *Motivação e Ginástica Artística no Contexto Extracurricular*. (Master's thesis). University of São Paulo, São Paulo, Brazil.

Lyle, J., Allison, M., & Taylor, J. (1997). *Factors influencing the motivations of sports coaches*. Edinburgh: The Scottish Sports Council Caledonia House.

Mallett, C., & Côté, J. (2006). Beyond winning and losing: guidelines for evaluating high performance coaches. *The Sport Psychologist, 20*, 213-221.

Massimo J., & Massimo S. (2013). *Gymnastics Psychology: the ultimate reference guide for coaches, athletics and parents*. New York: Morgan James Publishing.

Nista-Piccolo, V. L. (2003). Pedagogia dos esportes. In Nista-Piccolo, V. L. (Ed.), *Pedagogia dos esportes*. Campinas: Papirus.

Nunomura, M. (1998). Segurança na Ginástica Olímpica. *Motriz, 4*(2), 65-68.

Nunomura, M. (2001). *Técnico de Ginástica Artística: uma proposta para a formação profissional*. (Doctoral dissertation). State University of Campinas, Campinas, São Paulo, Brazil.

Nunomura, M. (2004). Formação profissional na ginástica artística e os modelos internacionais. *Revista Brasileira de Ciência e Movimento, 12*(3), 63-69.

Nunomura, M. (2005). Segurança na ginástica artística. In M. Nunomura, & V. Nista-Piccolo (Eds.), *Compreendendo a ginástica artística* (pp. 59-75). São Paulo: Phorte.

Nunomura, M., & Nista-Piccolo, V. L. (2003). A Ginástica Artística no Brasil: Reflexões sobre a Formação Profissional. *Revista Brasileira de Ciências do Esporte, 24*(3), 175-192.

Oliveira, M. S. (2010). *O panorama da ginástica artística masculina brasileira: um estudo histórico-crítico do período 2005-2008.* (Master's thesis). State University of Campinas, Campinas, São Paulo, Brazil.

Oliveira, M. S., & Bortoleto, M. A. C. (2011). Apontamentos sobre a evolução histórica, material e morfológica dos aparelhos da ginástica artística masculina. *Revista da Educação Física/UEM (Online), 22*(2), 283-295.

Olusoga, P., Butt, J., Hays, K., & Maynard, I. (2009). Stress in elite sports coaching: identifying stressors. *Journal of Applied Sport Psychology, 21*(4), 442-459.

Readhead, L. (1993). *Manual de entrenamiento de gimnasia masculina.* Barcelona: Paidotribo.

Rúbio, K., Kuroda, S., Montoro, F. C. F., & Queiroz, C. (2000). Iniciação esportiva e especialização precoce: as instâncias psicossociais presentes na formação esportiva de crianças e jovens. *Revista Metropolitana de Ciências do Movimento Humano, 1*, 52-61.

Samulski, D. (1992). *Psicologia do esporte: teoria e aplicação prática.* Belo Horizonte: Imprensa Universitária UFMG.

Simões, A. C., Bohme, M. T. S., & Lucator, S. (1999). A participação dos pais na vida esportiva dos filhos. *Revista Paulista de Educação Física, 13*(1), 34-45.

Smoleuskiy, V., & Gaverdouskiy, I. (1996). *Tratado general de lagimnasia artística deportiva.* Barcelona: Paidotribo.

Weinberg, R. S., & Gould, D (2001). *Fundamentos da Psicologia do Esporte e do Exercício.* São Paulo: Artmed.

Winterstein, P. (1992). Motivação, Educação Física e Esporte. *Revista Paulista de Educação Física, 6*(1), 53-61.

CHAPTER 4

CONTRIBUTIONS OF SPORT PSYCHOLOGY TO COMPETITIVE GYMNASTICS

Thomas Heinen[1], Pia Maria Vinken[2] & Konstantinos Velentzas[3]

[1]*University of Hildesheim - Institute of Sport Science (Germany).*
Correspondence to: thomas.heinen@uni-hildesheim.de

[2]*Leibniz University Hanover - Institute of Sport Science (Germany).*
Correspondence to: pia.vinken@sportwiss.uni-hannover.de

[3]*Bielefeld University - Department of Sport Science (Germany).*
Correspondence to: kostas.velentzas@uni-bielefeld.de

Acknowledgement:
The content of this chapter is largely based on Chapter 9 'Gymnastics psychology' in the book: *Gymnastics* (Handbook of sports medicine and science) edited by Dennis J. Caine, Keith Russell, and Liesbeth Lim, 2013, published by John Wiley & Sons, Ltd., and is reproduced here by kind permission of the publishers.

4.1 Introduction

When one watches a gymnastics competition, different actors, such as coaches, gymnasts, judges, or spectators will exhibit a lot of different behaviors. These behaviors are thought to result from the dynamic interplay of person acting in a particular environment with regard to specific task demands (Schack & Bar-Eli, 2007). For example, the behavior of a coach relies on previous observations of the performance of his/her gymnast/s, and the preparation of a particular gymnast may rely on factors such as his/her observation of the previous routine, his/her current arousal level or his/her current confidence level. The preparation itself may in turn influence the gymnasts' behavior in the upcoming routine (Cox, 2007; Salmela, 1983).

In gymnastics, the task demands are in principle defined by the competitive rules, the boundary conditions of the gymnastics apparatus, together with biomechanical and functional constraints related to an appropriate movement technique (Davids, Button, & Bennett, 2008). Task demands may vary from trial to trial, and being able to vary skill performance according to diverse influences is for instance an important characteristic of elite gymnasts (Prassas, Kwon, & Sands, 2006; Raab, de Oliveira, & Heinen, 2009). Furthermore, physiological factors such as height and weight, as well as psychological factors such as perceptions, cognitions, and emotions are thought to influence performance, and differences in these factors can lead to differences on how a person approaches a particular goal in gymnastics. Finally, physical factors that are related to the composition and structure of objects in the environment as well as social factors such as leading persons, social support, peer groups, or norms can have a strong influence on gymnast's behavior (Nitsch, 2009; Salmela, Petiot, & Hoshizaki, 1987).

Keeping the diverse factors just described in mind, the first and foremost goal in gymnastics psychology is to optimize the person-environment relationship with regard to a given task in order to support gymnasts' effort to optimize his/her actions to best suit the current circumstances of a given situation (Nitsch, 2009; Schack & Hackfort, 2007). One fundamental step would be to equip the gymnast with skills that may support this optimization process. It should be kept in mind, however, that influences of factors on each of the levels just mentioned may contribute to the development of certain problems, especially if they significantly influence the person-environment fit (Schack & Hackfort, 2007).

4.2 Psychological demands in high performance gymnastics

One major effort in sport psychology was to characterize a psychological profile for elite gymnasts in which selected psychological characteristics were identified that were thought to covary with gymnasts' expertise (Krane & Williams, 2006; Orlick & Partington, 1988). Research suggests, that elite gymnasts have for instance a high degree of self-confidence, are less anxious, are mentally tough, have a clear focus on the task, view difficult situations as challenging, are intrinsically motivated, attribute failures more to external events and are strongly committed to gymnastics, as compared to their less-skilled counterparts, or as compared to novices (Gould, Dieffenbach, & Moffett, 2002; Mahoney & Avener, 1977; Mahoney, Tyler, & Perkins, 1987; Spink, 1990). Empirical evidence furthermore indicates that differences in athletes' psychological characteristics may covary with factors such as skill level, competition level, gender, and cultural background (Cox, 2007; Mahoney & Avener, 1977). It is thus the right mixture of perceptions, cognitions, emotions, and behaviors in specific situations that influence the pathway to performance one gymnast might achieve. Several authors agree, that the systematic use of psychological skills and strategies may support this process (Fournier, Calmels, Durand-Bush, & Salmela, 2005). These skills and strategies should be learned and continually practiced, as well as integrated into gymnasts' physical preparation, and refined if necessary so that a gymnast is able to perform to his/her maximum potential (Arkaev & Suchilin, 2004; Cox, 2007; Velentzas, Heinen, Tenenbaum, & Schack, 2010).

Expert gymnasts usually exhibit a high ability in spatial orientation and (automatic) movement regulation (Bradshaw, 2004; Davlin, Sands, & Shultz, 2004; Raab, de Oliveira, & Heinen, 2009). Movement adjustments usually occur almost naturally with minimal conscious effort or attention. However, under some circumstances, movement skills appear to be suddenly changed (Grandjean, Taylor, & Weiner, 2002) or even lost by a gymnast (Day, Thatcher, Greenlees, & Woods, 2006). When suffering from such a 'lost-skill syndrome' gymnasts find themselves unable to perform a skill that was previously performed in an automatic manner. Such a loss of skill often results from a singular situation in which the gymnast performed a complex skill and lost spatial orientation during skill performance. Sometimes, this disorientation leads to a serious fall or even injury. This loss of skill can lead to significant changes on different levels. For instance, most gymnasts show a strong stress response when trying to perform a 'lost' skill, which usually leads to a complete avoidance of skill execution or breakdown in motor control. This stress response often comprises perceptual and attentional changes, heightened levels of cognitive and somatic anxiety, perceived loss of control, and negative self-talk. A loss of skill could imply a career-destroying potential for a particular gymnast, since this phenomenon seems to be very resistant to change (Day et al., 2006).

Apart from the gymnasts' personality, his/her psychological characteristics or specific problems such as the lost-skill syndrome, the active or passive presence of other people can have direct or indirect influences on the gymnast (Coté, Salmela, Trudel, Baria, & Russell, 1995). Elite gymnasts compete and train in a physical, social, psychological, and organizational environment that can have both facilitative and debilitative effects upon the achievement of ideal performance states, and one of the most influencing factors is without question the coach. Several researchers would argue that good coaches are able to develop gymnasts to their personal best (Arkaev & Suchilin, 2004; Jemni, 2011). However, coaches' work is a multidimensional and also a highly dynamic process. Coaches not only organize and manage training but also support and interact with the gymnasts before, during and after competition. They should furthermore deal with aspects such as parental influences, spectators, or gymnasts' personal concerns, as well as represent the sport of gymnastics, and fulfill expectations of committees, federations and others. Gymnasts are likely to perform better and they are more satisfied when the actual behavior of the coach and the behavior that is required in a particular situation are congruent with the behavior that the gymnasts prefer (Chelladurai, 1990). For instance, after a successful competition, members of a gymnastics team could prefer that their coach also has an eye on the social part of the sport activity. If the actual behavior (e.g., going out for a diner) is in line with the team norms than this is likely to have a positive effect on gymnasts' satisfaction which, seen in the long run, could potentially increase their effort in training. It may sound that the aforementioned attributes are very hard to adopt for a coach in the multidimensional and complex setting of gymnastics. However, it is stated that as it is a hard piece of work for a young gymnast to acquire the diverse gymnastics skills, it may also be a hard piece of work for a young coach to acquire the diverse attributes and characteristics that may support gymnasts to perform to their personal best.

4.3 Psychological interventions in gymnastics

It was already discussed that elite gymnasts possess certain (psychological) characteristics that make it possible for them to experience success in gymnastics. Empirical evidence highlights that psychological intervention programs are effective in developing and enhancing psychological skills, and thus are effective in enhancing gymnasts' performance (Hardy, Jones, & Gould, 1996). These intervention strategies may also help to cope with problems such as the lost-skill syndrome. However, using psychological methods in gymnastics training is not quite trivial and coaches are advised to apply state-of-the art knowledge on psychological methods in a person-centered approach when working with gymnasts on all ages (Schack & Bar-Eli, 2007). It could even be advisable to seek help from professional sport psychologists when implementing psychological methods in the daily training schedule. The general purpose of using psychological methods is to put oneself in an optimally aroused, confident and focused state immediately before as well as during routine execution. This aim, however, implies that the used methods have been developed in gymnastics training on a systematic basis leading to the intended changes in arousal, confidence or focus. Seen in the long run, it is argued that integrating psychological intervention programs in daily training is most effective if the gymnast is able to personalize and claim ownership of specific methods in such a way that they become useful strategies for him/her (Chase, Magyar, & Drake, 2005).

First and foremost, coaches are encouraged to develop training and competition plans together with their gymnasts. These plans should comprise the diverse individual goals, the steps and behaviors that are necessary to reach these goals as well as the steps that should be taken in case of emerging problems. For instance, it could be advisable to write down the behavioral steps that a gymnast could apply to refocus from a mistake such as falling down the balance beam. Using training diaries could be one way in implementing this strategy. Gymnasts' individual goals should be evaluated in a systematic way relative to the individual development of the gymnast, and refined if necessary and/or appropriate (Cox, 2007). A necessary precondition to implement such a strategy is that the gymnast is able to estimate his/her performance in a realistic way. One simple, yet effective intervention strategy is the so-called prediction training (Eberspächer, 2007).

This training approach can be easily and creatively applied in a wide range of different situations. The approach consists of four steps (see Figure 4.1). In the first step, the coach defines a specific task for a gymnast such as performing a back somersault ten times with a perfect landing. In the second step, the gymnast predicts the outcome when performing the task. He/she could for instance predict to perfectly perform and land the somersault in five out of ten times. In the third step, the gymnast executes the task and the coach counts the successful attempts. The fourth step comprises a reflection of

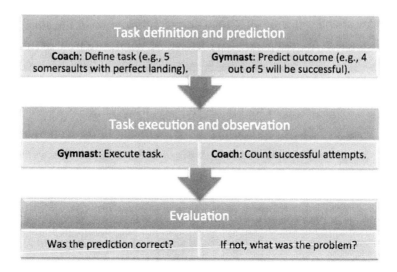

Figure 4.1: Basic structure and example of prediction training in gymnastics.

the gymnasts' task performance in relation to his/her prediction. The coach and the gymnast should discuss questions such as: Was the task too easy/too hard for the gymnast to achieve? Or: Was the prediction realistic in relation to the task demands and the gymnasts' abilities? The prediction training can be made more challenging by adding a time delay between task prediction and task execution or by adding diverse distractions such as cheering gymnasts. Prediction training can also be combined with the use of video technology.

Coaches are furthermore encouraged to integrate general psychological skills training programs into gymnasts' physical training on a regular basis. These programs should aim at teaching gymnasts different psychological methods such as imagery or relaxation to optimize different psychological skills. Each session of such training programs can address different psychological methods and psychological skills, such as relaxation techniques (e.g., awareness of abdominal breathing), self-talk techniques (e.g., using positive self-talk to cope with fear), focusing (e.g., shifting focus from narrow to broad), or imagery techniques (e.g., shifting imagery perspective from internal to external). From the authors own experience it is beneficial to begin integrating such a program in gymnastics groups at ages 11 to 13 for two times half an hour per week over a time period of six to seven months (Fournier et al., 2005).

One simple, yet quite effective method in order to deal with high levels of arousal is the so-called progressive muscular relaxation (Jacobson, 1938; Greenberg, 1996). Progressive muscular relaxation is used to reduce anxiety and stress by eliciting a relaxation response of the body. Usually gymnasts lie on their back in a quiet and comfortable place (Fig. 4.2). First, they try to induce some basic relaxation state by shifting their attention to their breathing. Afterwards they execute a particular sequence of tensing and relaxing their muscles. Therefore, the attention is initially focused in a specific body part (e.g., dominant forearm) and its corresponding muscles. Then the muscles of the body part are tensed for three to ten seconds. When relaxing the muscles after the tension phase the gymnast again focuses his/her attention on the body part for fifteen to twenty seconds and tries to feel how the previous tension vanishes. Then he/she shifts his/her attention to the next body part. The following sequence has been proven to be advantageous because it implies a good balance between duration of the sequence and muscles to activate: 1. dominant forearm and hand, 2. dominant upper arm and shoulder, 3. non-dominant forearm and hand, 4. non-dominant upper arm and shoulder, 5. face, 6. neck and upper thorax, 7. lower thorax and hips, 8. non-dominant thigh, 9. non-dominant shank and foot, 10. dominant thigh, 11. dominant shank and foot. The coach or a sport psychologist

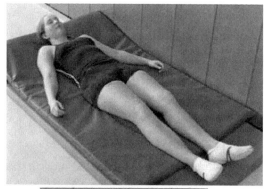

Figure 4.2: Different body positions when exercising progressive muscular relaxation in the gym (e.g., Jacobson, 1938).

can easily instruct the complete sequence when working with beginning gymnast. It may also be useful to integrate specific elements of progressive muscular relaxation into an imaginary journey. Specific templates can be found in the common sport psychology literature.

Most sport psychologists would argue, that psychological methods are most effective if they are adapted individually to each gymnasts' strengths and weaknesses. It may therefore be beneficial to assess the gymnasts' psychological strengths and weaknesses and use this to improve the application of already known or further methods. At this step it is recommended to consult a professional sport psychologist. Afterwards, selected psychological methods should be integrated into so called performance routines, since they are thought to be highly beneficial for performance stabilization and optimization in gymnastics (Cotterill, 2010).

Psychological methods are also often integrated into more complex intervention strategies, especially if the gymnast exhibits persistent problems. These intervention strategies usually incorporate relaxation training, imagery and other cognitive processes. For instance, a specific intervention strategy that can be particularly used to cope with fear and anxiety is called visual motor behavior rehearsal (VMBR; Suinn, 1994). There exist several different approaches to VMBR in the sport psychology literature. The most common application of VMBR in gymnastics consists of three phases. First, the gymnast relaxes his/her body. This is often achieved by applying strategies such as progressive muscular relaxation, autogenic training or alike. In the second phase, the gymnast imagines the task in which he/she experiences fear or anxiety (e.g., imagining a fearful dismount on the balance beam). During this phase the sport psychologist should support the gymnast by exploring his/her imagination by means of specific instructions/metaphors (e.g., imagining oneself as a dwarf performing the dismount on an oversized balance beam). It may also be advisable to increase or decrease the amount of anxiety gradually depending on the verbal and nonverbal reactions of the gymnast. The third phase comprises the execution of the task under realistic conditions. Depending on the task demands and the current mastery level of the task it may be advisable to use specific training aids in order to gradually increase the task difficulty (e.g., gradually reducing the width of the balance beams' take-off surface). Visual aids such as photo slides or video sequences of successful performances may also be helpful in the process of VMBR. Depending on the current situation and the gymnast, it may be necessary to pass through the second and third phase alternately, namely using imagery, practicing in the gym, using imagery again, practicing in the gym and so on.

4.4 Conclusion

The diverse behaviors observable in gymnastics result from the interplay of person acting in a particular environment with regard to specific tasks. A person-task-environment fit is a significant precondition for a gymnasts' optimization of actions in a particular situation (e.g., competition) and thus for the attainment of peak performance. There are several personality traits and psychological states that seem to be related to gymnasts' performance, development, and mental health. Continually practicing psychological skills and strategies may influence psychological states in the short run. These changes in psychological states may in turn lead to changes in personality traits in the long run, leading to enhancements in personality development, which should be considered positive in nature (Salmela, Petiot, & Hoshizaki, 1987).

In order to support gymnasts' development, effective coaching strategies should be applied. Effective coaching is characterized by an open communication and the presence of coaches' rewarding behavior for gymnasts' effort and performance. The coach and the gymnasts feel respect for one another and appreciate each other's roles. Elite gymnasts not only possess specific psychological states but also regulate complex skills more precise than their less-skilled counterparts.

Dramatic changes in psychological states are thought to be a potential precondition for movement errors, injuries or even for a loss of skill. Experienced gymnasts are far from being 'machines' that produce the same pattern of movement in every trial. Even if this might look so at first sight, biomechanical analyses usually reveal that there will always remain some trial-to-trial variability, and the question would be which (psychological) factors influence this variability and when does this variability support and when does it hamper performance.

It can finally be stated, that gymnastics coaches are advised to apply state-of-the art knowledge on psychological methods in a person-centered approach when working with gymnasts on all ages. Psychological methods can be thought of as a set of tools that gymnast could use to optimize his/her psychological states and in turn to optimize subjective and objective performance. To be effective, the methods should be practiced in a systematic and regular manner, and they should be integrated into physical training in such a way, that the gymnast is able to personalize and claim ownership of the methods for his/her individual needs.

References

Arkaev, L. I., & Suchilin, N. G. (2004). *How to create champions. The theory and methodology of training top-class gymnasts.* Oxford: Meyer & Meyer Sport.

Bradshaw, E. (2004). Target-directed running in gymnastics: a preliminary exploration of vaulting. *Sports Biomechanics, 3*(1), 125-144.

Chase, M. A., Magyar, M., & Drake, B. M. (2005). Fear of injury in gymnastics: self-efficacy and psychological strategies to keep on tumbling. *Journal of Sports Sciences, 23*(5), 465-475.

Chelladurai, P. (1990). Leadership in sports: a review. *International Journal of Sport Psychology, 21,* 328-354.

Coté, J., Salmela, J., Trudel, P., Baria, A. & Russell, S. (1995). The coaching model: a grounded assessment of expert gymnastic coaches' knowledge. *Journal of Sport and Exercise Psychology, 17*(1), 1-17.

Cotterill, S. (2010). Pre-performance routines in sport: current understanding and future directions. *International Reviews of Sport and Exercise Psychology, 3*(2), 132-153.

Cox, R. H. (2007). *Sport psychology. Concepts and applications.* New York, NY: McGraw-Hill.

Davlin, C. D., Sands, W. A., & Shultz, B. B. (2004). Do gymnasts "spot" during a back tuck somersault? *International Sports Journal, 8,* 72-79.

Davids, K., Button, C., & Bennett, S. (2008). *Dynamics of skill acquisition. A constraints-led approach.* Champaign, IL: Human Kinetics.

Day, M. C., Thatcher, J., Greenlees, I., & Woods, B. (2006). The causes of psychological responses to lost move syndrome in national level trampolinists. *Journal of Applied Sport Psychology, 18,* 151-166.

Eberspächer, H. (2007). *Mentales Training. Das Handbuch für Trainer und Sportler* (7. Aufl.) [Mental training. A handbook for coaches and athletes (7th ed.)]. Munich: Copress.

Fournier, J. F., Calmels, C., Durand-Bush, N., & Salmela, J. H. (2005). Effects of a season-long PST program on gymnastic performance and on psychological skill development. *International Journal of Sport and Exercise Psychology, 3,* 59-77.

Greenberg, J. S. (1996). *Comprehensive stress management* (5th ed.). Madison, WI: Brown & Benchmark.

Gould, D., Dieffenbach, K., & Moffett, A. (2002). Psychological characteristics and their development in olympic champions. *Journal of Applied Sport Psychology, 14,* 172-204.

Grandjean, B. D., Taylor, P. A., & Weiner, J. (2002). Confidence, concentration, and competitive performance of elite athletes: a natural experiment in olympic gymnastics. *Journal of Sport & Exercise Psychology, 24,* 320-327.

Hardy, L., Jones, G., & Gould, D. (1996). *Understanding psychological preparation for sport. Theory and practice of elite performers.* Chichester: John Wiley & Sons.

Jacobson, E. (1938). *Progressive relaxation* (2nd ed.). Chicago: Chicago University Press.

Jemni, M. (2011) (Ed.). *The science of gymnastics.* New York: Routledge.

Krane, V., & Williams, J. M. (2006). Psychological characteristics of peak performance. In J. M. Williams (Ed.), *Applied sport psychology: personal growth to peak performance* (pp. 207-227). New York, NY: McGraw-Hill.

Mahoney, M. J., & Avener, M. (1977). Psychology of the elite athlete: an exploratory study. *Cogntive Therapy and Research, 1*(2), 135-141.

Mahoney, M. J., Tyler, J. G., & Perkins, T. S. (1987). Psychological skills and exceptional athletic performance. *The Sport Psychologist, 1*, 181-199.

Nitsch, J. R. (2009). Ecological approaches to sport activity: a commentary from an action-theoretical point of view. *International Journal of Sport Psychology, 40*, 152-176.

Orlick, T., & Partington, J. (1988). Mental links to excellence. *The Sport Psychologist, 2*, 105-130.

Prassas, S., Kwon, Y.-H., & Sands, W. A. (2006). Biomechanical research in artistic gymnastics: a review. *Sports Biomechanics, 5*(2), 261-291.

Raab, M., de Oliveira, R. F., & Heinen, T. (2009). How do people perceive and generate options? In M. Raab, J. G. Johnson, & H. Heekeren (Eds.), *Progress in Brain Research: vol. 174. Mind and motion: the bidirectional link between thought and action* (pp. 49-59). Amsterdam, NL: Elsevier.

Salmela, J. H. (1983). Understanding gymnastic performance. In L.-E. Unestahl (Ed.), *The mental aspects of gymnastics* (pp. 47-53). Örebro: Veje Förlag.

Salmela, J. H., Petiot, B., & Hoshizaki, T.B. (Ed.) (1987). *Psychological nurturing and guidance of gymnastic talent*. Montreal: Sport Psyche Editions.

Schack, T., & Bar-Eli, M. (2007). Psychological factors in technical preparation. In B. Blumenstein, R. Lidor, & G. Tenenbaum (Eds.), *Psychology of sport training* (2nd ed., pp. 62–103). Oxford: Meyer & Meyer.

Schack, T. & Hackfort, D. (2007). Action-theory approach to applied sport psychology. In G. Tenenbaum, & R.C. Eklund (Eds.), *Handbook of sport psychology* (3rd ed., pp. 332-351). Hoboken, NJ: Wiley.

Suinn, R. M. (1994). Visualization in sports. In A. A. Sheikh, & E. R. Korn (Eds.), *Imagery in sports and physical performance*. Amityville, NY: Baywood.

Spink, K. S. (1990). Psychological characteristics of male gymnasts: differences between competitive levels. *Journal of Sports Sciences, 8*, 149-157.

Velentzas, K., Heinen, T., Tenenbaum, G., & Schack, T. (2010). Functional mental represenation of volleyball routines in german youth female national players. *Journal of Applied Sport Psychology, 22*(4), 474-485.

CHAPTER 5

THE CONTENT OF RHYTHMIC GYMNASTICS COMPETITION ROUTINES

Lurdes Ávila-Carvalho[1], Catarina Leandro[2] & Eunice Lebre[3]

[1] *Porto University - Sports Faculty (Portugal).*

[2] *University Lusófona of Porto - Faculty of Psychology, Education and Sport (Portugal).*

[3] *International Gymnastics Federation.*

Correspondence to: lurdesavila@fade.up.pt

5.1 Introduction

The first time that rhythmic gymnastics (RG) groups took part in the Olympic Games was in 1996 in Atlanta. Since then, the performance standard, in international competitions have been increasingly demanding. The RG code of points is the universal guideline for the sport, implemented by the International Gymnastics Federation (FIG) RG technical committee. The code of points is, at bottom, the guiding document that determines how the routines are designed, implemented and also how they should be interpreted. This document has two main goals: (1) standardize the technical requirements for the sport, allowing a more objective evaluation, and (2) guide the sport development both rewarding technical elements that contribute to the sports evolution, and penalizing those which are considered not harmful to the RG evolution.

This reference document is submitted to periodic changes (usually at the beginning of each Olympic cycle). These change use to include an increase in composition requirements and drills difficulty (Lisitskaya, 1995). The study of the talent prognosis and sports performance has been one of the main topics within the sports sciences (Schiavon, Paes et al., 2011). Related to this topic it is essential to study the content of competition routines, since RG in the performance is associated to three main factors: the quality of the composition, the quality of the execution, and also the quality of the artistic performance. Thus, we believe that is fundamental to develop an analysis mainly focused on the efficacy and athletic performance.

The most part of the technical studies in gymnastics has been based on code of points. However, according to Bauch (2001) the analysis of competition routines should be more focused on the qualitative content of the routines than in the rules of the code of points. According to the author, only in this way it is possible to develop different approaches analyzing competition routines. In this way it is possible to extend the knowledge in RG using a dual source of information: on the one hand, using the official rules based on the code of points (Vidal, 1997), and on the other hand, based on the sports sciences contributes. According to Vidal (1997) the competition routine evaluation is made from a subjective judgment or assessment by a group of experts who evaluate the quality of the routines according to pre-established rules. Despite the subjective component of gymnastics evaluation, an objective analysis (both in quantitative and qualitative terms) of the difficulty elements allows a better understanding and interpretation of the rules by the coaches, providing further data about the gymnasts evolution the and about the accuracy of initial plan.

The purposes of this chapter are: (i) To go deep and contextualize the characteristics groups competition routines in RG, and (ii) to analyze the studies made with RG groups.

5.2 Characteristics of rhythmic gymnastics

We could identify a lot of RG definitions, according to different authors' point of view (Vidal, 1997). One of the definitions that, in our opinion, are one of the widest and that include all the important components of RG was developed by Laffranchi (2005). According to this author, RG is a constant search for beauty, an explosion of talent and creativity, in which the body expression and technical virtuosity grow together, in a harmonious motion. According to Vidal (1997) the most part of the studies in RG have been based on the apparatus handling analysis, on the gymnasts' physical and technical capacities and abilities, or also based on the aesthetic and artistic dimension of the sport.

If we put our focus on the routine we will recognize body movement (natural, full, fluid and rhythmic) as a base, coordinated with the handling of different apparatus (rope, hoop, ball, clubs, and ribbon) (Vidal, 1997). According to this author, when the execution quality is studied also the interpretation of the composition must be taken into account (mastery and virtuosity) that, by its aesthetic character, reveal qualities associated with grace, harmony, rhythm, and beauty. It is from the combination between the quality of the routines composition and the execution that gymnasts achieve the source of aesthetic pleasure that is the great attraction for show in this sport (Vidal, 1997). According to Lebre (1993) scarcity of studies on RG with regard to the technical analysis of the routines associated with constant evolution of both composition and execution requirements has justified the limited number of studies in the sport. According to the author this shortage hinders the comparison of results for those who want to devote themselves to study the routines content.

The RG is characterized by promoting different motor skills in both dynamic general coordination (displacements, jumps, rotations, and balances) and in the different ways of apparatus handling (lead, rotate, throw, catch ...) (Vidal, 1997). The motor tasks in RG have a high level of complexity and risk (Lebre, 1993; Vidal, 1997). The movements are not purely mechanical. They include an emotional charge that allows feelings expression (Vidal, 1997). In an overall analysis of RG, it is not enough to study the movements' technique (Vidal, 1997). The contents selection to compose competition routines in RG is usually made by the coach (Lebre, 1993). This selection is done according to 3 main factors: the Code of Points requirements, the age group and the technical level of the gymnasts. The interpretation of the composition is conducted and supervised by the coach during the training process. However, if we analyze this interpretation as a final product, i.e. during the competition, this is from the entire responsibility of the gymnast.

In Figure 5.1, we present, in a summarized way, the composition requirements for RG groups routines in the last two Olympic cycles and Olympic period that began in 2013.

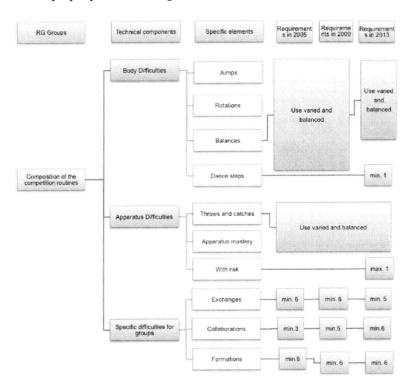

Figure 5.1: Composition requirements for the RG groups competition routines.

The main goal for this set of rules for routines construction is to standardize requirements (Lebre, 1993) allowing to establish quantitative and qualitative difference between various compositions. The requirements outlined in Figure 5.1 are used for all types of exercises, i.e. it is applicable for any kind of apparatus (rope, hoop, ball, clubs and ribbon) regardless if the exercise is to be performed with only one type of apparatus (e.g., five hoops) or with two different types (e.g., two ribbons and three ropes).

We can observe in Figure 5.1 that the difficulty elements in RG group routines are divided into 3 technical components: body difficulties, apparatus difficulties and specific difficulties for groups. These 3 main technical components are subdivided into different types of specific technical elements. The body difficulty elements are divided in jumps, rotations, balances, and dance steps. In the last cycles there was no minimum amount required for each type of element. For the Dance steps the minimum requirement for the 2013-2016 Olympic cycle is one sequence with a minimum duration of eight seconds.

The apparatus difficulty elements are divided in apparatus mastery, throws and catches and elements with risk. Apparatus mastery has specific characteristics for each apparatus although the other two groups have common execution characteristics for all apparatus in RG. As minimum requirement it is said that each RG group routine should include a minimum of one element with risk. The specific group elements are divided in exchanges, collaborations and formations. Although, minimum requirement for formations has been maintained for the lasts cycles, the number of exchanges will have a slightly decrease in the cycle 2013-2016 requirements. The collaborations have been the specific group elements that had registered an increase in number, what, in our opinion, has contributed to evolution in quality of the RG groups' routines.

These changes in the code of points may have basically three different characteristics: 1) they can be organizational; 2) they can be structural or 3) it can be morphological. 1) As organizational change we can point out the case of the difficulty elements flexibility / waves that disappeared as body technical group in code of points after 2013, but were redistributed among the remaining groups depending on their mechanical characteristics. Thus the flexibilities / waves were relocated in other technical groups according to the main mechanical function: rotation or balance, even if the support base is a part of the body other than the foot. 2) Structural, as in the case of dance steps and elements of risk that appears as a compulsory requirement in the routines composition in 2013 code of points. Or 3) Morphological, when refer to the changes in the requirement criteria level for the body difficulties. Those changes are sometimes so wide that the results confrontation form studies made in different Olympic cycles are not easy (Lebre, 1993) In addition to the general rules for routines composition described above there are also general rules regarding the quality of execution and artistic interpretation. Regarding the execution we can find some common definitions how the body movements, apparatus movements' and specific groups' movements should be. These common definitions allow an objective evaluation for gymnasts and groups during the competitions.

The construction and artistic interpretation of RG routine has as main goal to project an emotional image for the public and present a choreographic idea with an expressive interpretation guided by three fundamental aspects: music, artistic image and expressivity (Barel, Péchillon et al., 2012).

The artistic performance refers to the ability of the gymnast or group to turn a technically well-structured composition in an artistic performance, where the expressive interpretation, musicality and the relation with the partners, all together have a key role for the success (Heward, 2012). In the official rules, there are precise quantitative and qualitative guidelines to evaluate the artistic component in RG routines.

5.3 Rhythmic gymnastics competition routines content

From the current research we can say that the majority the studies on the RG routines content were developed based on the technical body (64% - 14 studies). Among all studies found about RG, 32% (seven studies) were based on the apparatus technique. Finally, only one study (4%) had as goal analyzing the artistic content of RG routines (see Appendix).

When analyzing the studies about the routines content according to the type of competition (individual or groups) we found that 59% (13 studies) were developed in groups, 36% (eight studies) were for individual and that 5% (one study) refers to the comparison between the two specialties. When we analyze the conclusions and considerations presented on studies, we noted that (see Appendix):

1. The body difficulties presented in RG routines (individual and groups) tend to be identical among different compositions analyzed (Bobo & Sierra, 1998; Lebre, 2007; Ávila-Carvalho, Corte-Real et al., 2008; Ávila-Carvalho, Palomero et al., 2009b; Ávila-Carvalho & Lebre, 2011; Ávila-Carvalho, Palomero et al., 2011a; Ávila-Carvalho, Klentrou, Palomero et al., 2012) showing some lack of variety.

2. Jumps have been the most used movements in RG routines (Ávila-Carvalho, Corte-Real et al., 2008; Ávila-Carvalho & Lebre, 2011; Ávila-Carvalho, Palomero, & Lebre, 2011a; Ávila-Carvalho, Klentrou, Palomero et al., 2012) and pivots / rotations have been the least used (Caburrasi & Santana, 2003; Ávila-Carvalho, Palomero et al., 2009b; Salvador, 2009; Ávila-Carvalho, Klentrou, Palomero et al., 2012). However jumps are part of the group with less variety and pivots form the group with a higher variety (Lebre, 2007; Ávila-Carvalho, Klentrou, Palomero et al., 2012).

3. There has been observed an increase in the number of exchanges performed in the RG group routines during the last Olympic cycle (Ávila-Carvalho, Palomero et al., 2009b; Ávila-Carvalho, Klentrou, Palomero et al., 2012; Sierra & Bobo, 2000; Vidal, 1997).

4. The group routines performed with one or two apparatus have shown differences in technical body content (Vidal, 1997), regarding the choice of collaborations (Ávila-Carvalho, Palomero et al., 2010a, 2011b; Ávila-Carvalho, Klentrou, & Lebre, 2012) and the apparatus technique (Ávila-Carvalho, Palomero et al., 2010b).

5. The higher number of risk elements have been a characteristic of the high-level gymnasts and groups (Lebre, 1993; Ávila-Carvalho, Palomero et al., 2010a, b; Ávila-Carvalho, Klentrou, & Lebre, 2012).

6. There has been observed a high variety in the choice of apparatus elements (Cardoso, 2009; Ávila-Carvalho, Palomero et al.,

2011b), however, the clubs routines have shown a lower variety compared to the other apparatus (Vidal, 1997; Ávila-Carvalho, Klentrou, & Lebre, 2012).

7. There has been a prevalence in the use of criteria rather in the throws than in the catches (Ávila-Carvalho, Corte-Real et al., 2008; Ávila-Carvalho, Palomero et al., 2009a, 2010a, 2011b; Ávila-Carvalho, Klentrou, & Lebre, 2012).

5.4 Final considerations

To know in a methodical and systematic way the routines (content and how they are organized) of the gymnasts and the groups that get the best results at international level let us: 1) identify one direction and a guideline to the work, since this analysis can identify the path development of the gymnasts or groups, and 2) approach the interpretation of the code of points and the strategies used by reference coaches in RG. The study of the routines content should cover not only the technical elements: body, apparatus, and groups specificities, but also as the execution artistic dimension since it is from the combination of all these factors that is possible to point out a comprehensive and integrated analysis of the RG routines composition. Finally, we believe that further studies based on the routines could influence the development programs and also influence the experimental designs used in scientific research in RG.

References

Avila-Carvalho, L., Corte-Real, A., Araújo, C., Botelho, M., Lacerda, T., & Lebre, E. (2008). Artistic value score for Rhythmic Gymnastics group exercises in Portimão 2007 World Cup Series. In F. A. J. Cabri, D. Araújo, J. Barreiros, J. Dinis, & A. Veloso (Eds.), *Book of abstracts of the 13th annual congress of the european college of sport science, sport science by the sea* (pp. 150-151). Lisbon: FMH.

Ávila-Carvalho, L., Corte-Real, A., Araújo, C., Botelho, M., Lacerda, T., & Lebre, E. (2008). Difficulty score for Rhythmic Gymnastics group exercises in Portimão 2007 World Cup Series. In F. A. J. Cabri, D. Araújo, J. Barreiros, J. Dinis, & A. Veloso (Eds.), *Book of abstracts of the 13th annual congress of the european college of sport science, sport science by the sea* (pp. 149-150). Lisbon: FMH.

Ávila-Carvalho, L., Klentrou, P., & Lebre, E. (2012). Handling, throws, catches and collaborations in elite group rhythmic gymnastics. *Science of Gymnastics Journal, 4*(3), 37-47.

Ávila-Carvalho, L., Klentrou, P., Palomero, M. d. L., & Lebre, E. (2012). Analysis of the technical content of elite Rhythmic Gymnastics group routines. *The Open Sports Sciences Journal, 5*, 146-153.

Avila-Carvalho, L., & Lebre, E. (2011). A Dificuldade dos Exercícios Individuais e de Conjuntos de Elite de Ginástica Rítmica. *Motricidade. II Simpósio Internacional de Performance Desportiva, 8*(S1), 77-78.

Ávila-Carvalho, L., Palomero, M. d. L., & Lebre, E. (2009a). Artistic score for Rhythmic Gymnastics group routines in 2008 Portimão World Cup Series. *Motricidade, 5*(3), 94.

Ávila-Carvalho, L., Palomero, M. d. L., & Lebre, E. (2009b). Difficulty score for Rhythmic Gymnastics group routines in Portimão 2008 World Cup Series. *Motricidade, 5*(3), 93.

Ávila-Carvalho, L., Palomero, M. d. L., & Lebre, E. (2009c). Difficulty score in group Rhythmic Gymnastics. Portimão 2007/2008 World Cup Series. *Palestrica Mileniului III. Civilizatie si sport, Anul X, 3*(37), 261-267.

Ávila-Carvalho, L., Palomero, M. d. L., & Lebre, E. (2010a). Apparatus difficulty in groups routines of elite rhythmic gymnastics at the Portimão 2009 World Cup Series. *Science of Gymnastics Journal, 2*(3), 29-42.

Ávila-Carvalho, L., Palomero, M. d. L., & Lebre, E. (2010b). Mastery and risk with throw in apparatus difficulty of elite rhythmic gymnastics groups. *Anais do II Seminário Internacional de Ginástica Artística e Rítmica de Competição (SIGARC)*, 195-201.

Ávila-Carvalho, L., Palomero, M. d. L., & Lebre, E. (2011a). Body difficulty score (D1) in group Rhythmic Gymnastics in Portimão 2009 World Cup Series. In FGP (Ed.), *Da Prática à Ciência. Artigos do 2º e 3º Congresso de FGP* (pp. 105-113). Lisboa.

Ávila-Carvalho, L., Palomero, M. d. L., & Lebre, E. (2011b). Estudio del valor artístico de los ejercicios de conjunto de Gimnasia Rítmica de la Copa del Mundo de Portimão 2007 y 2008. *Apunts. Educación Física y Deportes, 1.er trimestre(103)*, 68-75.

Ávila, L. (2001). Estudo do nível de dificuldades dos exercícios de Ginástica Rítmica nos Jogos Olímpicos de Sydney 2000. (Degree Thesis). Universidade do Porto, Faculdade de Ciências do Desporto e de Educação Física, Porto.

Barel, A., V., Péchillon, F., & Carrée, J. (2012). Question d'artisque, l'Artistique en question. *GymTechnic, 78*, 8-14.

Bauch, R. (2001). *Controversial Topic: "Code de Pointage"*. Retrieved May 20, 2010, from http://www.gymmedia.com/FORUM/agforum/bauch_code_e.htm.

Bobo, M., & Sierra, E. (1998). Una nueva propuesta de dificultades corporales en gimnasia rítmica deportiva. *Libro de resúmenes del VI Congreso de Educación Física e Ciencias do Deporte dos Países de Lingua Portuguesa*. Deporte e Humanismo en clave de Futuro.

Bobo, M., & Sierra, E. (2003). Estudio de las repercusiones de los cambios de código de puntuación en la composición de los ejercicios de gimnasia rítmica en la técnica corporal. Retrieved September 3, 2011, from http://www.cienciadeporte.com/congreso/04%20val/pdf/p3.pdf.

Caburrasi, E. F., & Santana, M. V. (2003). Análisis de las dificultades corporales en los Campeonatos Europeos de Gimnasia Rítmica Deportiva Granada 2002. Retrieved December 9, 2009, from http://www.efdeportes.com/efd65/grd.htm.

Cardoso, A. I. (2009). *Avaliação do Nível de Dificuldade de Aparelho dos Exercícios Individuais de Competição de Ginástica Rítmica das Ginastas Portuguesas dos Escalões Juvenil e Júnior*. (Master's thesis). Porto University, Sports Faculty, Porto.

Heward, L. (2012). *Artistic Perfomance in Gymnastics*. Lousanne: International Gymnastics Federation.

Laffranchi, B. (2005). O treinamento de Alto Rendimento na Ginástica Rítmica. In P. U. SportsFaculty (Ed.), *Planejamento, Aplicação e Controle da preparação técnica da Ginástica Rítmica: Análise do Rendimento técnico alcançado nas temporadas de competição*. (Doctoral dissertation). Porto University, Sports Faculty, Porto.

Lebre, E. (1993). *Estudo comparativo das exigências técnicas e morfofuncionais em Ginástica Rítmica Desportiva*. (Doctoral dissertation). Porto University, Sports Faculty, Porto.

Lebre, E. (2007). Estudo da dificuldade dos exercícios apresentados pelas ginastas individuais na Taça do Mundo de Portimão 2007. *Actas do 2º Congresso Nacional de Formação da Federação de Ginástica de Portugal*, 301-306.

Lisitskaya, T. (1995). Datos básicos sobre la gimnasia rítmica. In E. Paidotribo (Ed.), *Gimnasia Rítmica* (pp. 9-21). Barcelona.

Salvador, G. (2009). *Avaliação do Nível de Dificuldade Corporal dos Exercícios Individuais de Competição de Ginástica Rítmica das Ginastas Portuguesas da Categoria de Juvenil e de Júnior*. (Master's thesis), Porto University, Sports Faculty, Porto.

Schiavon, L. M., Paes, R. R., Moreira, A., & Maia, G. B. M. (2011). Training phases and volume of training for Brazilian female gymnasts in Olympic Games (1980-2004). *Motricidade, 7*(4), 15-26.

Sierra, E., & Bobo, M. (2000). Estudio de la variable técnica en los ejercicios de conjunto en gimnasia rítmica deportiva. *Actas del Primer Congreso de la Asociación Española de Ciencias del Deporte*, 171-180.

Vidal, A. (1997). *La Dimensión Artística de la Gimnasia Rítmica Deportiva*. (Doctoral dissertation), Universidad de Vigo, Faculdade de Bellas Artes Departamento de Expresión Artística, Pontevedra.

Appendix - Summary table

On the following pages, we present a summary table with the studies we found in literature about the RG competition routines content (see chapter text above for details).

Summary table with the studies about the RG competition routines content

Authors (Year)	Title	Sample (n)	Level	Specialty (Apparatus/ Specificity) /Age group	Content	Statistical anlaysis	Main conclusions and comments
Lebre (1993)	Comparative study of the technical and morph functional requirements in Rhythmic Gymnastics	184	International (WC Athens 1991) National (Qualification competition for the national team 1992)	Individuals (rope, hoop, ball, clubs/ national level gymnasts vs. international level gymnasts) / Seniors	Routine duration, distance traveled, displacement velocity. Body technique, Apparatus technique	Descriptive, Correlation, Anova (Sheffé F-test)	The International level gymnasts registered longer routines, smaller distance traveled and lower displacement velocity than the national level gymnasts. The international level gymnast's routines presented a higher difficulty and risk index when compared to the national level gymnasts. The routines of the international level gymnasts presented specific characteristics for each apparatus (routine length, distance traveled and number of elements), which was not registered for national level gymnasts.
Vidal (1997)	The Artistic Dimension of the Rhythmic Gymnastic	17	International (Spain NC 1994 e 1995)	Groups (5 gym. 2TA) /Seniors, (5 gym. SA)/Juvenile, (5 gym. SA)/ Juniors, (6 gym. FH, 6 gym. SA)/Infants, (6 gym. FH)/minis	Artistic Dimension	Descriptive	The culminating moments of the routines were coincident with successive throws, predominance same body actions except routines with 2 different apparatus or odd number of gymnasts. The conduct of attention was predominantly dispersed; the apparatus exchanges were in small number to an average of 5, formations were with high variety but predominantly geometrical figures and lines. The displacements had low variety; large amplitude movements were the most frequent followed by those that include wave; there was great variety in the apparatus technique being ribbon and clubs the poorest. Personality traits of the routines were based more on expressive than on the originality.
Bobo & Sierra (1998)	A new proposal for the Body difficulties in Rhythmic Gymnastics	8	International (EC Greece 1997)	Individuals (Hoop) /Seniors	Body Technique	Descriptive	Routines difficulty level were different but nor the final scores nor the final ranking did not reveal these differences. The gymnasts tended to have the same difficulties with the consequent lack of variety.
Sierra & Bobo (2000)	Study of technique variable in group exercises in Rhythmic Gymnastics	72	International (WC Seville 1988, Spain NC Zaragoza 1998, EC Budapest 1999)	Groups (5 balls, 3 hoops/2 ribbons, 10 clubs) /Seniors, (5 ribbons)/Juniors, (3 hoops/ 4 clubs)/ Juveniles, (6 balls)/Infants	Body Technique	Descriptive and frequence distribution	The most performed actions were those not linked to body difficulties. From the actions were the exchanges that had higher frequency of occurrence. The average duration of actions with difficulty was 3:58 seconds (min.2 and max. 4). The difficulties were homogeneously distributed throughout the 150 second duration of the routine.
Ávila (2001)	Study of the difficulty level of the Rhythmic Gymnastics routines in Sydney 2000	12	International (OG Sydney 2000)	Individuals (rope, hoop ball and ribbon) /Seniors	Body Technique	Descriptive	The changes that CoP (2001) introduced (in relation to the CoP 1997) forced major changes in the routines composition including the inclusion of a greater number of jumps in the rope routines, greater number of flexibilities in ball routines, greater number of pivots in the ribbon routines and a balanced use of body difficulty in hoop routines. These changes made it difficult to obtain the maximum score in Technical Value and allowed easier to distinguish the level of the gymnasts. These changes encourage the specialization of gymnasts per apparatus and promote a more rigorous assessment (by the requirement to present competition sheets).

Study	Aim	N	Event	Sample	Variables	Statistics	Results
Bobo & Sierra (2003)	Study the impact of the code of points changes in the rhythmic gymnastics routines regarding the body technique	96	International (EC Zaragoza 1999, EC Geneve 2001, WC Budapeste 2003)	Individuals (rope, hoop, ball, clubs and ribbon) /Seniors	Body Technique	Descriptive and Variance analysis	There was an increase in the total number of body difficulties as well as in its variety in routines exercises performed after changes in 2003 CoP.
Caburrasi & Santana (2003)	Analysis of the Body Difficulties in the Rhythmic Gymnastics European Championships Granada 2002	32	International (EC Granada 2002)	Individuals (rope, hoop, ball, clubs) /Seniors	Body Technique	Descriptive, percentages, correlation	With CoP (2001) there was an increase in the number of difficulties. The jumps were the most used followed by the flexibilities and balances. The pivots were those who had lower utilization. The routines Technical Value was correlated with the level of difficulty elements and not with the its number.
Lebre (2007)	Study of routines difficulty of the individual gymnasts at Portimão 2007 World Cup	240	International (WCup Portimão 2007)	Individuals (rope, hoop, clubs, ribbons)/Seniors	Body Technique	Descriptive, percentages	For the 4 apparatus analyzed the same choice of body difficulties was registered: Jumps - higher number of "jeté with turn" balances - higher number with trunk at the horizontally with different positions of the free leg, pivots - higher number with free leg in front or side, flexibilities / waves – higher number with trunk at horizontal or back and with the free leg high. The jumps were the group that showed a lower variety in the choice of the difficulties; pivots were the difficulties group which presented a higher variety.
Ávila-Carvalho et al. (2008)	Artistic value score for Rhythmic Gymnastics group exercises in Portimão 2007 World Cup Series	38	International (WCup Portimão 2007)	Groups (5 ropes vs. 3 hoops/ 4 clubs) /Seniors	Apparatus Technique	Descriptive, percentages	Throws – Higher number of apparatus mastery related to the throws when compared to the catches; however in the routines with different apparatus higher number of mastery elements related to the catches. Collaborations - In exercises with 5 ropes was higher number of collaborations without throw and with risk while in 3 hoops/4 clubs routines there were a higher number of collaborations with simple throw. Apparatus Specific technique - in 5 ropes there was a higher number of jumps through the rope and in 3 hoops / 4 clubs there was a higher number of handlings.
Ávila-Carvalho et al. (2008)[16]	Difficulty score for Rhythmic Gymnastics group exercises in Portimão 2007 World Cup Series	38	International (WCup Portimão 2007)	Groups (5 ropes vs. 3 hoops/ 4 clubs) /Seniors	Body Technique	Descriptive, percentages	Jumps - higher number of "jeté with turn"; Balances - higher number with trunk horizontally with different positions of the free leg, pivots - higher number with free leg in front or side. Flexibilities / waves - higher number with trunk at horizontal and the leg high. The body elements the most used were individual body difficulties, but when it was in connection with body difficulties, wer the jumps the groups more chosen.
Cardoso (2009)	Assessment of the Apparatus Difficulty Level of Individual Routines in Portuguese Rhythmic Gymnastics Gymnasts of the Junior and Juvenile Age Group	336	National (Portugal NC 2008 and 2009)	Individuals (rope, hoop, ball) /Juvenile e Junior	Apparatus Technique	Descriptive, percentages	In 2009, there was a general increase and a more balanced distribution of the Apparatus difficulty groups than in 2008. There was a greater variety in the choice of the apparatus difficulty elements. The changes to the CoP will be reflected in the trends, evolution and enrichment of the sport.

Author	Title	N	Level	Sample	Variables	Analysis	Main Results
Salvador (2009)	Assessment of the Body Difficulty Level of Individual Routines in Portuguese Rhythmic Gymnastics Gymnasts of the Junior and Juvenile Age Group	300	National (Portugal NC 2008 and 2009)	Individuals (rope, hoop, ball) /Juvenile e Junior	Body Technique	Descriptive	In 2009 NC there was a general increase in jumps value and a decrease in the balances and pivots values in the competition routines. There was also a decrease in both the total amount of difficulty elements performed and in the number of difficulties from the non-compulsory group. There has been an increase in the number and value of compulsory body difficulties groups. Pivots were the body group less used in routines forb all apparatus analyzed.
Ávila-Carvalho, Palomero & Lebre (2009a)	Artistic score for Rhythmic Gymnastics group routines in 2008 Portimão World Cup Series	32	International (WCup Portimão 2008)	Groups (5 ropes vs. 3 hoops/ 4 clubs) /Seniors	Apparatus Technique	Descriptive, percentages	Throws – Higher number of apparatus mastery elements performed in connection with throws compared to the catches; however the exercises with 2 different apparatus registered a higher number of mastery elements connected to catches. Collaborations - The routines with 5 ropes had a higher number of collaborations with risk while the routines with 3 hoops / 4 clubs had a higher number of collaborations with simple throw. Apparatus specific technique - in 5 ropes routines there was a higher number of jumps through the rope and in 3 hoops / 4 clubs routines there was a higher number of "handlings".
Ávila-Carvalho, Palomero & Lebre (2009b)	Difficulty score for Rhythmic Gymnastics group routines in Portimão 2008 World Cup Series	32	International (WCup Portimão 2008)	Groups (5 ropes vs. 3 hoops/ 4 clubs) /Seniors	Body Technique	Descriptive, percentages	Jumps - higher number of "jeté with turn; Balances - higher number with trunk horizontally with different positions of the free leg, pivots – higher number of "fouettes" in 3 hoops / 4 clubs routines and also with free leg in front or side. Flexibilities / waves - higher number with the trunk at horizontal and the leg high. The body elements the most used were the jumps and the flexibility / waves. The exchanges were mostly performed without body difficulties, but when it was in connection with body difficulties, were the jumps the group more chosen in rope routines and flexibilities in hoops/clubs.
Ávila-Carvalho, Palomero & Lebre (2009c)	Difficulty score in Group Rhythmic Gymnastics. Portimão 2007/2008 World Cup Series	70	International (WCup Portimão 2007 and 2008)	Groups (5 ropes vs. 3 hoops/ 4 clubs) /Seniors	Body Technique	Descriptive, percentages	Jumps - higher number of "jeté with turn; Balances - higher number with trunk horizontally with different positions of the free leg; Pivots – higher number of "fouettes" in 2008 routines and with free leg in front or side in 2007 routines; Flexibilities / waves - higher number with the trunk at horizontal and the leg high. The body elements the most used were the jumps (2007 e 2008) despite in 2008 a slightly decrease in the jumps number and a slightly increase in pivots number were registered. The exchanges were mostly performed without body difficulties, but when it was in connection with body difficulties, were the jumps and flexibilities the groups more chosen (2007 and 2008) although there was a decrease in the use of body difficulties in the exchanges in 2008, which means an increase in the number of exchanges body without difficulty.

Ávila-Carvalho, Palomero & Lebre (2010a)	Apparatus difficulty in groups routines of elite rhythmic gymnastics at the Portimão 2009 World Cup Series	26	International (WCup Portimão 2009)	Groups (5 hoops vs. 3 ribbons/ 2 ropes)/ Seniors	Apparatus technique	Descriptive, Wilcoxon test	Throws – Higher number of apparatus mastery with throws compared to those performed with catches. The throws were performed mainly during a jump. Catches - were executed mostly during an element of rotation in 3 ribbons / 2 ropes and without hands on 5 hoops routines. Risks – Higher number of risk elements in 5 hoops than in 3 ribbons / 2 ropes routines; Higher number of simple risk elements in 5 hoop routines and with 1 additional rotation in 3 ribbons/2 ropes routines. In both type of routine the change in body axis was the criterion used to increase the value of the risks, however higher in 5 hoops than in 3 ribbons/2 ropes. Specific apparatus technique - in 5 hoops there was a higher number of "handling", while in ribbon and there was a higher number of spirals and serpentines. Collaborations - In 5 hoops routines there was a higher number of collaborations with risk while in 3 ribbons/2 ropes there was a higher number of collaborations with simple throw.
Ávila-Carvalho, Palomero & Lebre (2010b)	Mastery and risk with throw in apparatus difficulty of elite rhythmic gymnastics groups	26	International (WCup Portimão 2009)	Groups (5 hoops vs. 3 ribbons/ 2 ropes)/ Seniors	Apparatus technique	Descriptive, percentages	Mastery with throw – Higher number in 5 hoops routines; Mastery without throw - Higher number in 3 ribbons/2 ropes routines. The throws were performed mostly during a jump (in both type of routine), however the catches were performed mostly during one rotation element 3 ribbons/2 ropes and without hands in 5 hoops. Risks – performed simple in 5 hoops routines and with additional rotations in 3 ribbons/2 ropes routines. In both type of routine the change in body axis was the criterion more used to increase the risk elements value
Ávila-Carvalho & Lebre (2011)	Difficulty Level of Individual and Group Exercises in Elite Rhythmic Gymnastics	19 (Gr) 74 (Ind)	International (WCup Portimão 2007)	Individuals (Rope and hoop) vs. Groups (5 ropes e 3 hoops/ 4 clubs)/ Seniors	Body Technique	Descriptive, percentages	Jumps - Higher number of "jeté with turn". Balances - higher number with trunk horizontally with different positions of the free leg; Pivots - the higher number of pivots performed with free leg in front or side; Flexibilities/waves - higher number with trunk horizontally with leg high; In individual routines there also a high number of scales with back bend trunk. The body element groups more used were the jumps (Gr and Ind in rope) and flexibilities/waves in the individual routines with hoop. The balances were the difficulty elements less in the individual routines and in group 5 ropes routine; In the hoop/clubs group routines the pivots were the body elements less used.
Ávila-Carvalho, Palomero & Lebre (2011a)	Body Difficulty Score (D1) in Group Rhythmic Gymnastics in Portimão 2009 World Cup Series	26	International (WCup Portimão 2007)	Groups (5 hoops vs. 3 ribbons/ 2 ropes)/ Seniors	Body Technique	Descriptive, percentages	Jumps - Higher number of "jeté with turn". Balances - higher number with trunk horizontally with different positions of the free leg; Pivots - the higher number of pivots performed with free leg in front or side; Flexibilities/waves - higher number with trunk horizontally with leg high; The body element groups more used were the jumps. The exchanges were performed mostly without body difficulties; when in connection with difficulty the body element chosen was mainly jumps

Author	Title	n	2TA	SA	Variables	Statistics	Results
Ávila-Carvalho, Palomero & Lebre (2011b)	Artistic Value Assessment of Rhythmic Gymnastics Group Routines in Portimão 2007 and 2008 World Cup	35	International (WCup Portimão 2007 and 2008)	Groups (5 ropes vs. 3 hoops/ 4 clubs – 2007 vs. 2008) /Seniors	Apparatus technique	Descriptive, percentages	Throws – Higher number of mastery elements linked with throws than with catches; however in 2008 there was an increase in the number of throws and a decrease of catches. Collaborations - higher number of collaborations without throw in 2007, while in 2008 there was a higher number of collaborations with risk in 5 ropes routines. On 3 hoops/4 clubs routines there was a higher number of collaborations with throw but with a decrease in 2008; in 2008 there was an increase in the number of collaborations with risk. Apparatus specific technique - in 5 ropes there was a higher number of jumps through the rope with an increase in 2008; in 3 hoops/4 clubs there was a higher number of hoop "handlings" which remained from 2007 to 2008 and a higher number of mills in clubs in 2007 and 2008 despite having been a decrease in 2008 and an increase of handlings in the same year
Ávila-Carvalho, Klentrou, Palomero & Lebre (2012)	Body elements technical and level evaluation in high level Rhythmic Gymnastics groups routines	126	International (WCup Portimão 2007 to 2010)	Groups (ranking first half vs. ranking second half)/ Seniors	Body Technique	Descriptive, Kolmogorov-Smirnov and t-test	The body difficulties followed a pattern consistent with the position of the groups in the rankings. The main characteristics of the routine composition were the prevalence of exchanges and of jumps and the poor use of rotations. The jumps were the technical group with less variety and rotations the technical group with greater variety. The limited variety in the choice of body a difficulty in RG routines composition make them dull and compromises its artistic evaluation.
Ávila-Carvalho, Klentrou & Lebre (2012)	Handling, throws and collaborations in Elite Rhythmic gymnastics	126	International (WCup Portimão 2007 to 2010)	Groups (rope vs. hoop vs. clubs vs. Ribbon / Finalists vs. Non finalists) /Seniors	Apparatus Technique	Descriptive, Kolmogorov-Smirnov , Kruskal-Wallis, Mann-Whitney, Linear regression	The hoop routines were those more balanced in the use of different apparatus techniques and the clubs routines were the poorest, which was probably due to be a "double apparatus". According to analysis, the success in competition could be explained by: a high volume of training hours (43%), high use of criteria for throws (6%) and the use of collaborations with risk (16.5%). This risky form of apparatus technique in groups with greater success in competition requires foresight coincidence that is more difficulty in the case by the loss of visual contact with the apparatus.

Legend: EC – European Championship, WCup – World Cup, WC – World Championship, NC – National Championship, OG – Olympic Games, Gr – Groups, Ind – Individuals, CoP – Code of Points, FH – Free hands, SA – Same Apparatus, 2TA – 2 Type of Apparatus, n – number of routines, gym - gymnast

CHAPTER 6

QUALITATIVE VIDEO ANALYSIS AS A PEDAGOGICAL TOOL IN ARTISTIC GYMNASTICS

Marco Antonio Coelho Bortoleto[1] & César Jose Duarte Peixoto[2]

[1] *University of Campinas - Physical Education Faculty (Brazil).*
Correspondence to: bortoleto@fef.unicamp.br

[2] *Technical University of Lisbon - Faculty of Human Kinetics (Portugal).*
Correspondence to: cpeixoto@fmh.ulisboa.pt

Acknowledgement:
This chapter presents part of the results of a study, which was financed by the "The Coordination of the Development of the Staff of Higher Learning" (CAPES – Process: BEX 4975/09-0), the institution to which we owe our thanks. We also thank Prof. Dr. Milton Shoiti Misuta of the Biomechanical and Instrumentation Laboratory of the Physical Education Faculty (University of Campinas) for the suggestions on our manuscript.

6.1 Introduction

> "The qualitative approach will produce a description of movement in non-numerical terms (...). Qualitative evaluations of performance should be based on the analyst's ability to recognize the critical features of the skill" (Kreighbaum & Barthels, 1996, p. 5).

A qualitative analysis of videos is an important tool that can be used throughout the processes of teaching and learning, as well as in the training of motor skills in artistic gymnastics (AG). The use of this tool has grown significantly during the last two decades due to the development of specific computer systems (software / computer programs).[1]

This kind of analysis represents a simplified system for observation, registering, and analysis of motor skills and techniques obtained from images of daily training or competition (Hauw & Durand, 2007). The parameters that make up the qualitative descriptive analysis of body movements differ in relation to the objectives of motor skills being analyzed, as well as in relation to the characteristics of the sport, with the goal of obtaining data which will enable the immediate adjustment of distinct technical aspects. Therefore, this resource presents itself as an important tool for coaches of different sports modalities where the technical execution represents a fundamental aspect of the performance (Pozzo & Studeny, 1987; Sarmento, 2004).

In literature we find various studies that discuss the qualitative analysis (Knudson & Morrison, 2001; Hay & Reid, 1988). As men-

---

[1] It is worth remembering that during the 1980s and 1990s videos were mainly VHS (flexible magnetic tape) in analogical format. Thanks to the exponential technological advancement in the subsequent decades, these images were gradually substituted by digital images, recorded in different devices and formats. Today, the recording devices include HD (High Definition) format and HS (High Speed) format, offering data of significantly greater quality.

tioned by Hay (1993), the analyzed facts primarily come from videos or photographic sequences[2] (see Fig. 6.1), obtained without the rigor and precision that characterize the quantitative analysis, especially the biomechanical analysis (Kreighbaum & Bartels, 1996; Smith, 1982).

Figure 6.1: Four-frame sequence obtained from the original video.

As such, the results of the analysis cannot be used in the formulation of the theoretical-mathematical models and neither can they aspire to the precision and objectivity that characterizes scientific studies (Yeadon & Brewin, 2003), which produce, in general, results that are difficult to visualize and which require complex interpretations.
In general, and according to Sarmento (2004):

---

[2]Currently, there are different digital camera models for the recording of high speed sequences, or even high definition videos, facilitating even more the achievement of quality data.

> *"Understanding the architecture of task levels of segmental movement enables one to highlight the particularities and the diverse levels of functional explanation, of the motor unit, of the muscle, of the movement of one limb, the place from which the concept emerges, as expressed by Robb (1972). The "critical component" represents the most difficult and critical parts of execution, or (the parts) which provoke us to greater concentration of attention. The observation of the task should equally observe the context of its execution in relation to the existence of cinestesical factors, which can cause segmental errors of execution" (Sarmento, 2004, p. 172).*

In this way, the qualitative analysis of the gymnastics skills, even when using technological resources such as software, computers, and digital cameras, remains a methodological procedure usually utilized in non-laboratory situations, that is, during the AG daily training or competition, without the need for special equipment or complex systems, resulting in a tool that offers rapid "feedback" to the interested parties, usually coaches or sports practitioners (Boyer, 2008). This practicality permits that the results obtained may be immediately applied in the practice arena, a fact that draws the attention of many specialists in this particular modality (Bortoleto, 2004; Arkaev & Suchilin, 2004). In a certain way, and maintaining due distances (technological, temporal, etc.), these observations corroborate the affirmations made by Sands (1984):

> *"Videotaping and filming athletes is very important for analyzing technique and providing feedback for learning. You should acquire a high-speed film camera and a videotape machine (...). The videotape gives instantaneous feedback to the coach and athlete (...). I consider the computer an almost indispensable adjunct to training and skill analysis" (Sands, 1984, p. 57).*

As we mentioned beforehand, one of the main principles that direct this kind of analysis is the technological and conceptual simplicity, a condition that does not impede a systematic recording method. In fact, it is exactly its practicality that enables the registration of a large number of data, in relation to one or more gymnasts, allowing for daily observation, and therefore, technical development. The constant and practical recording of data even permits a comparison intra or inter-subjects in a common training session, or competition, or over a longer period of time. It is possible, for example, to create databases for each gymnast in order to provide a detailed observation of his/her technical development, as well as for the sharing of information between coaches whether they are present, or from a distance via internet.

During the last two decades the attention that the analysis of qualitative videos has received among specialists has led to the creation of various specific software, some of them free (open source), as in the case of KINOVEA[3], others gratuitous (freeware), such as SkillCapture - SkillSpector[4], and many others that can be purchased, such as Dartfish (Switzerland). A list of computer software that permit the qualitative analysis of human movement has become consistently more extensive[5], offering ever more sophisticated and precise resources, whose creators range from enthusiastic programmers and research groups, to multi-nationals from the technological sports sector. In some cases, such as that of GASP GYM[6], the computer pro-

---

[3] See http://www.kinovea.org, a program that some AG coaches have been using.
[4] Developed by a group from South Denmark University – SDU (http://video4coach.com) and used successfully in the International School of Gymnastics of Ollerup (Denmark).
[5] Among the best-known, we highlight COMODATE SWINGER - Webbsoft – UK (http://www.webbsoft.co.uk); TEMPLO: Professional Video Analysis Software – Mar Systems – UK (http://www.mar-systems.co.uk); SportsCAD MOTION ANALYSIS – Germany (http://www.sportscad.com); CODAMOTION – UK (http://www.codamotion.com); EAGLE EYE Digital Video (USA) (http://www.eagleeyedv.com).
[6] GASP GYM (UK) (http://www.gaspsystems.com).

gram was developed specifically for use with AG, including unique tools according to the characteristics and needs of this modality. The relevance and practicality of this instrument can be observed in the suggestion that the United States Olympic Committee made to the professionals who participated in the development of Olympic coaches program, as we can note in the words of Riewald (2009):

> *"Just because you use a computer as part of your review process does not mean you need to engage in complicated or quantitative analyses. Every year more and more software packages become available to help you, as coaches, review and categorize video" (Riewald, 2009, p. 2).*

During the last few years, based upon our experience and study of several biomechanical (Karácsony & Čuk, 2005) and pedagogical models (Peixoto, 1991, 1997; Moreira, 1988)[7] we have identified some suggestions in order to maintain a minimum of criteria for a systematic analysis of the videos, which as whole, facilitate the recording and processing of data (images), as well as the visualization of the results by the interested parties (coaches, gymnasts, judges, students, among others). Such suggestions are derived from the repeated application of this kind of motor skills analysis, which requires greater technical detail, even in a qualitative perspective. In this case, some suggestions offered by Wilson and Corlett (1995) as well as Smouleuskiy and Gaverdouskiy (1991) were considered[8].

---

[7]This study analyzed "Barani out" (in Trampoline terms), in the following modalities: Floor and Vault AG, Trampoline, Double Mini-Trampoline (Moreira & Peixoto, 2004, p. 139-164).

[8]The suggestions mentioned here are the result of an ongoing research project begun in 2010 in a partnership with the Gymnastics Research Group (FEF-UNICAMP) and the Lisbon Technical University (FMH - Sports Lab - CEAD), to compare the acrobatic actions executed on different elastic surfaces (SpE), seeking to comprehend the process of learning transference, as well as the possible applications of SpE in different acrobatic training situations.

In summary, the contributions we subsequently present will attempt to approximate even more the theoretical knowledge employed in the technical analysis, as suggests Carr (1998), to the practice of the professionals of AG, who, due to their intense routine of work, need practicality so that the regular recording becomes viable and so that this tool might become part of their daily activities, offering relevant information for the improvement of their activities.

6.2 The different levels of analysis

For a qualitative analysis that may occur when there is the intention to carry out a scientific study in biomechanics, the quality of the data is fundamental. This means that distinct variables, such as distance, height and angle (Carr, 1998), definition, speed of capture (frames per second), can facilitate, render more difficult, or even invalidate the analysis (Karácsony & Čuk, 2005). Therefore, systematic registers should combine the use of the best equipment possible, and the most precise calibrations (distance, focus, height, angulations, etc.) allowing for a more detailed analysis, and thus more clear and consistent results.

We should recognize that the objective of the analysis may vary from a simple need to review the execution of an exercise or an element in reduced velocity, or slow motion, to a more refined frame by frame, such as executed by Estapé (2002). In this context it is possible, and sometimes necessary, to analyze videos or sequences of images obtained without systematic preparation, or even prior planning, in function of the objectives, as it happens in competitions. However, this is not the recommended context.

Experience shows us that in some cases, coaches have the habit of filming their gymnasts during competitions in order to analyze the images later. On the other hand, other coaches choose to record different training sessions, with the intention of comparing different performances, or even with the intent of showing the gymnasts the mistakes which are often repeated.[9]

Once these general principles are observed, we understand that the analysis can occur on three distinct levels, as described below:

a) Global analysis: An ample description, from the initial body position (preparation) until the end of the skill execution[10], with spatial movement registered graphically in four quadrants (front, back, below and above), highlighting the observable mechanical aspects (angle segmental alignment, segmental dislocation, rotation direction and of the body in its totality). It is also possible to estimate the position and trajectory of the centre of mass, although not with precision. In general, this is the most common form of analysis offered by software in amateur sports. More sophisticated analyses require professionals and specialized equipment.

As a part of the global analysis, the textual register of the objective of the action is also recommend (Carr, 1998), as well as the main external conditions (sun, wind, type of surface, temperature, illumination, etc.), and also a descriptive-textual analysis of the relationship between the components of the action and its constraints (Peixoto, 1991), a function available in some software, such as KINOVEA.

---

[9]In 2010 we were able to observe the use of this tool in the daily activities at the AG Center training on National Institute of Sport (INSEP) in Paris (France), place where the AG French National Team works. In this location, several cameras and televisions permit the coaches and the gymnasts themselves to review the exercises and to collect data for future analysis.

[10]Carr (1998, pp. 137-139) describes the principal phases of movements and their respective "key-elements", information which can contribute to a more efficient qualitative analysis.

In order to facilitate the image record that we have just listed we suggest the projection of a grid (or a "mask" - see Fig. 6.2), similar to the one offered by the Templo program of the Mar System business, with axis and markers of vertical and horizontal dislocation upon the sequence of selected frames. The grid permits one to visualize the dislocation in pre-established units of measurement. In this way the registration stands out and can be recorded (in JPG format, for example), or printed separately from the original image. Moreover, the

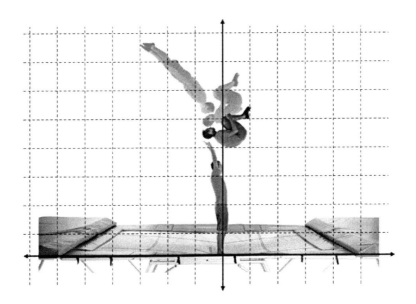

Figure 6.2: Grid application and image sequence upon axis.

mask permits a clear view of the errors detected in the analysis (such as, for example, a lack of pointing of the feet and a slight separation of the legs in Figure 6.2, frames 3 and 4, respectively), as well as the observation of the amplitude of movement and the positioning of the body segments in each skill phase: preparation, execution and finalization (Peixoto, 1991). It is also possible to compare the results of quantitative analysis with "ideal" models, elaborated by quantitative studies or even models built by virtual simulators such as those created by Yeadon in the field of gymnastics (Yeadon, Kong, & King, 2006).

Finally, the global analysis can be an important tool for judges training, not only by enabling the repeated visualization in slow motion, but above all, by permitting the preparation of videos (already judged) with highlighted explanations, the value of the each executed element and the failures in execution.

b) Detailed analysis: In this second level, which is not always available in the more simple computer programs, the objective is a clearer analysis from the separate visualization of the distinct frames, seeking more details in the segmental movements performed in the skill main phases. Sophisticated programs such as Codamotion or Dartfish permit an agile assembly of a sequence of overlapping frames, providing an important means for displaying "frozen" for one or more motor skills.

This observation allows one to deduct, albeit speculatively, or in an inaccurate manner, the consequences of the movement in the phases or following movements (Carr, 1998). In general, the detailed analysis is used to visualize the "takeoff" and "landing" phases, as suggested by Arkaev and Suchilin (2004), as well as a few "key points" in the "execution phase" such as the moment when the gymnasts begin some kind of segmental action which causes a dislocation upon one of the axis (rotations) (Fig 6.3; Hay & Reid, 1988).

Qualitative video analysis in artistic gymnastics. 109

In this case, the selection of the frame(s) which will be analyzed is of fundamental importance, and the specialist (coach, judge, or gymnast) is responsible for these decisions, which necessitates that this person have a thorough knowledge of the movement in analysis (Carr, 1998).

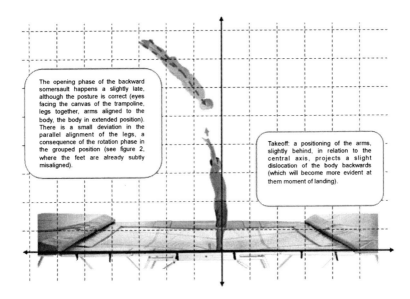

Figure 6.3: Detailed analysis of two frames: start and opening phase of backwards somersault.

The focus of a certain frame or a reduced number of frames is important for the detection of subtle errors during the gymnastic skills, which are often imperceptible without the use of audiovisuals, even to great specialists in the area of gymnastics. As a matter of fact, in a sport such as AG, it is precisely these small technical errors that can cause great problems (failure, execution error, accidents, etc.). Therefore, a detailed observation, in some cases, represents a fundamental mechanism for the identification of error, and in consequence, a means of facilitating the athlete's understanding with regard to where he/she should modify his/her skill, seeking to correct the error.

It is possible, as well, to calculate the duration of the determined phases of movement, given the quantity of frames, which is valuable information, considering the importance of the speed of skill execution which make up the AG repertoire, noting that the time and amplitude of the movement are aspects that can generate penalizations according to the Code of Points or even lesions to the athlete when they compromise precise execution.

c) Linear or sequential: In this third level, we propose a selection of frames of greater relevance, arranging them in a sequence for linear analysis, one frame juxtaposed with another. This resource allows for visual comparison of body movements (trajectory, alignment, etc.) through time, as seen in Estapé (2002). In the case of acrobatics, this resource has shown itself to be fundamental during the analysis of the rotations of the transversal axis (somersaults). In the Swinger software (Pro 2.0 version), for example, there is a similar option called "Multi-frame Windows".

In all the levels of analysis proposed above, it is recommended that one checks the need to introduce new variables or to prescient some of those indicated according to specific needs. For example, in sport modalities where the technical component follows specific and rigorous parameters, as in the case of artistic gymnastics, one may analyze, for example: the position of the feet (pointed or flexed during the execution), the leg position during the rotations, the angular position between certain body segments, the approximate trajectory of the center mass (center of gravity), or even the presence or absence of the flexing of the articulations of the knees during the landing phase.

However, we cannot forget that this is a qualitative analysis, whose graphic record upon the images is done a posteriori without the same precision and rigor that scientific studies require. Yet this does not mean that the possible analyses are not interesting to coaches or gymnasts as we have discussed before.

It is also important to pay attention to the positioning of the camera(s). Whenever possible, it is recommended that the cameras have a stable support, such as a tripod upon a stable surface (directly on the ground[11]), and that this tripod is adjustable for angle and height and at the angle and plane which will permit the most distinct view (Knudson & Morrison, 2001), in order to orient the camera perpendicular to the skill to be analyzed. In gymnasiums it is recommended that the cameras are attached walls, or in low-traffic areas, avoiding accidents or the need of displacement, and consequently, new calibration.

6.3 Final considerations

We understand that the qualitative analysis of videos permits one to efficiently study different aspects of motor skills, facilitating the comparison of the technical execution, especially in the context of training or competition. Furthermore, it is possible to compare a live situation with the theoretical models proposed by the code of points or even by the scientific studies and computer simulators. This kind of procedure also permits each professional to establish different parameters of recording and analysis, making the process even more specific,

---

[11] It is common to place the tripod upon the floor area, an elastic surface that can oscillate and cause distortions or diminish the quality of the images captured.

which, according to Wei, Zhi-Hong, and Xia-Wen (2009), is fundamental for the coach's work in AG.

From our point of view, the applicability of the distinct modes of recording and analysis (from the global to the most detailed) allows greater speed, and therefore greater quantity of information (feedback) about the technical training process. Certainly, the existing computer software offer different tools, which, together with the experience of the professionals in the AG area, make of this technological support an even more powerful instrument.

We understand that the different forms of visualization of the images (slow motion camera, frame by frame analysis,...), as well as the recording, the printing (on paper, for example), the possibility of freezing/marking the main frames detecting the moments where the technical errors are produced, make the qualitative analysis an even more useful instrument for AG. In this sense, the incorporation of the mask (grid), makes is so that the computer tools are more visual, as we can observe in the KINOVEA program, for example.

Therefore, as we consider the great importance of qualitative video analysis to those who work in the sports training area, we should recognize that should also be a part of the knowledge offered throughout their initial education[12]), perhaps as a first approximation to the biomechanical studies[13], where the knowledge of the mechanical variables, as well about the methods (for data collection or analysis), use

---

[12] Qualitative analysis has been used in the undergraduate program in the disciplines "EF445 Artistic Gymnastics" and "EF465 Training in Artistic Gymnastics" on Physical Education Faculty – UNICAMP (Brazil), demonstrating excellent results, both in the moment of explanation and discussion of the techniques specific to the modality, as well as during the process of students elaborating pedagogical proposals.

[13] In terms of Arkaev & Suchilin (2004, p. 384), a "biomechanical-pedagogical" approach.

more strict and sophisticated criteria, as we see in "Interaction Model Instruments" proposed by Peixoto (2010). This expectation is better explained by Carr (1998):

> *"When you observe elite athletes performing a skill you have a frame of speed, rhythm, power, body positions and other characteristics that make up a quality performance. This helps you understand the basic standards of technical movements in the technique of the skill you intend to teach" (Carr, 1998, p. 135).*

Finally, we hope that other professionals comprehend the contribution that the qualitative video analysis offers, especially for daily training and in the formation of specialized athletes, constituting an important ally for the qualification and optimization of the learning process and the improvement of the skill techniques used in AG.

References

Arkaev, L. I., & Suchilin, N.G. (2004). *Gymnastics: how to create champions.* Oxford: Meyer & Meyer Sport.

Bortoleto, M. A. C. (2004). *La lógica interna de la Gimnasia Artística Masculina (GAM) y estudio etnográfico de un Gimnasio de alto rendimiento.* (Doctoral dissertation). Universidade de Lleida: Lleida.

Boyer, E. (2008). *Expert video modeling with video feedback to enhance gymnastics skills.* (Master's thesis). University of South Florida: Florida.

Carr, G. (1998). *Biomecânicas dos esportes.* São Paulo: Manole.

Estapé, E. T. (2002). *La acrobacia en Gimnasia Artística: su técnica y su didáctica.* Barcelona: Editorial Inde.

Hay, J. G., & Reid, J. G. (1988). *Anatomy, mechanics, and human motion* (2nd ed.). Englewood Cliffs, NJ: Prentice Hall.

Hay, J. G. (1993). *The biomechanics of sports techniques* (4th ed.). Englewood Cliffs, NJ: Prentice Hall.

Hauw, D., & Durand, M. (2007). Situated analysis of elite trampolinists' problems in competition using retrospective interviews. *Journal of Sports Sciences,* 25(2),173-183.

Karácsony, I., & Čuk, I. (2005). *Floor Exercises*. Sangvincki: Ljubljana, STD.

Knudson, D., & Morrison, C. (2002). *Qualitative analysis of human movement* (2nd ed.). Champaign, IL: Human Kinetics.

Kreighbaum, E., & Barthels, K. M. (1996). *Biomechanics: a qualitative approach for studying human movement* (4th ed.). Allyn & Bacon: London.

Lees, A. (2002). Technique analysis in sports: a critical review. *Journal of Sports Sciences, 20*(10), 813-828.

McPherson, M. (1990). Systematic approach to skill analysis. *Sports Science Periodical on Research Technology in Sport, 11*(1), 1-10.

Moreira, M., & Peixoto, C. (2004). Análise das Interacções de Três Técnicas Gímnicas em Modalidades Diferenciadas. In V. Ferreira, & P. Sarmento (Eds.), *Formação Desportiva Perspectivas de Estudo nos Contextos Escolar e Desportivo* (pp. 139-164). Faculdade Motricidade Humana: Lisbon.

Moreira, M. (1998). *Analise das interacções de três técnicas gímnicas em modalidades diferenciadas*. (Doctoral dissertation). Universidade Técnica de Lisboa. Faculdade de Motricidade Humana (FMH), Lisboa.

Peixoto, C. (1991). *Similaridades motoras em desportos gímnicos observação de factores de sucesso em atletas de níveis competitivos diferenciados*. (Doctoral dissertation). Faculdade Motricidade Humana, Universidade Técnica de Lisboa.

Peixoto, C. (1997). *Sistemática das actividades desportivas: modelos e sistemas de análise do desempenho desportivo*. Editorial da Universidade Técnica de Lisboa. ISEF: Lisboa.

Peixoto, C. (2010). Technical Development. How coaches understand movements. Performance Indicators. *Acts of Coordination Motor habilities in Science Research, International association of Sport Kinetics* (pp. 49-54). Józef Pilsudski of Physical Education Warsaw. Faculty Physical Education and Sport, Akademicka 2 (Poland).

Pozzo, T., & Studeny, C. (1987). *Théorie et pratique des sports acrobatiques*. Paris: Editorial Vigot.

Riewald, S. (2009). Video analysis and applications in sport. *CSCSUSOC Performance Technology and Biomechanics Olympic Coach, 21*(2). Retrieved from: http://www.scribd.com/doc/33835108/Video-Analysis-in-Sport.

Robin, J. F., & Hauw, D. (1998). *Actualité de la recherché en activités gymniques et acrobatiques* (n. 39). Paris: EPS.

Sands, B. (1984). *Coaching women's gymnastics*. Champaign, IL: Human Kinetics.

Sarmento, P. (2004). *Pedagogia do desporto e observação*. Editorial da Universidade Técnica de Lisboa - Lisboa: ISEF.

Smith, T. (1982). *Gymnastics - a mechanical understanding*. Londres: Editorial Hodder and Stoughton.

Smoleuskiy, V., & Gaverdouskiy, I. (1991). *Tratado General de Gimnasia Artística Deportiva*. Barcelona: Editora Paidotribo.

Wei, L. W., Zhi-Hong, Y., & Xia-Wen, Y. (2009). A kinematical analysis on You Yanan's straight forward somersault with double twist and grip on horizontal bar. *Journal of Beijing Sport University, 32*(8), 121-129.

Wilson, J., & Corlet, E. N.(1995). *Evaluation of human work. A practical ergonomics methodology*. Bristol: Taylor and Francis.

Yeadon, M. R., & Brewin, M. A. (2003). Optimised performance of the backward longswing on rings. *Journal of Biomechanics 36*, 545-552.

Yeadon, M. R., Kong, P. W., & King, M. A. (2006). Parameter determination for computer simulation model of a diver and a springboard. *Journal of Applied Biomechanics, 22*, 167-176.

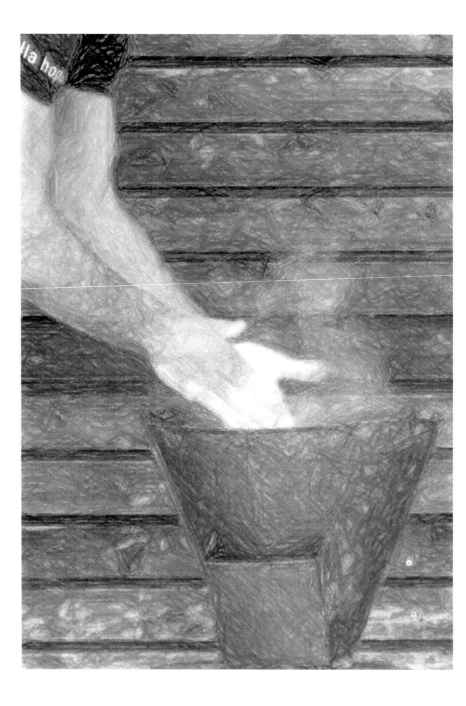

CHAPTER 7

GYMNASTICS: A GAME OF RULES

Jean-François Robin

Institut National du Sport, de l'Expertise et de la Performance (INSEP, France)
Correspondence to: jean-francois.robin@insep.fr

7.1 Introduction

In the gymnastic and acrobatic activities, the regulations of the game are called the "Code of Points". The Code of Points includes the rules of gymnastics. Its development is a long process, which is deeply ingrained in our social history. Questions arise, such as which rules to use when doing gymnastics, and which type of gymnastics to use and teach at schools today? In this article, we try to answer these main questions. The code of points is considered as a tool to be adapted according to the teacher's educational interests, according to the specific didactic intensions of the activity (risk-taking versus control), and according to the developments observed in gymnastic and acrobatic activities.

The Code of Points allows experts to evaluate a long "sequence of movements". At school the purpose is different. At school, the motor skill level of young gymnasts (pupils) decreases essentially in terms of gymnastic and acrobatic actions (sharing). Pupils need an adapted evaluation. The diversity of gymnastic motor skill level in pupils is at stake and the rules of gymnastics are designed to emphasize it.

7.2 Sociological characteristics of gymnastics

To understand the regulations of a sports activity, it is necessary to place it into its context, i.e. the field of practice. As gymnastics originates from a military tradition to train conquering soldiers, it was first used to represent force. It was static, including postures and attitudes. It taught strength, courage, righteousness, or self-sacrifice. After World War II, gymnastics became more and more dynamic and acrobatic. Run-ups were favored to do acrobatics but it was not well mastered because of spartan material conditions. It was only in the

80s that a more acrobatic and dynamic gymnastics developed. Since then, gymnastics has been part of acrobatic activities including trampoline, tumbling, diving, freestyle, and acrobatic skiing. Goirand (1996) for instance showed that gymnastics changed from an elegant, compulsory, team, and general-purpose activity to a free, individual, specialized, and risk taking activity.

Nowadays, gymnastics has developed in different ways (Goirand, 1994). For instance, a lot of children often start at a very young age (baby gym). One can observe a peak at the age of nine until adulthood, while the number of participants decreases after puberty (Robin, 1998). The strongest decrease in participation can be found at secondary school level (when children are between 11 and 16 years old). The activity does not seem to appeal to pupils at school when it is taught in a traditional way. If teachers want to make gymnastics attractive to their pupils, they have to find other innovative forms of practice.

The forms of practice are also very diversified, from leisure gymnastics or fitness gymnastics to high performance gymnastics, from one hour to 35 hours of weekly training. There are for instance more than half a million people who are devoted to this activity in France in school federations. Today, gymnastics in France and worldwide represents more than 80% of women; this is the reason why it is often stated that "gymnastics is a prepubescent female physical activity". The interest of a reflection about the sociological characteristics of gymnastics lies in the adequacy between the educational proposals and the social representations of the activity. It is also a question of understanding the social and technical transformations of practice in more detail in order to better address pupil's needs.

Finally, studying populations of gymnasts allows to adapt the regulations of gymnastics, which would enable better adaptions to the different levels of practice. But first this work requires a preliminary didactic analysis.

7.3 Interventions in sport

This reflection is akin to the one developed in the technology of physical and sporting activities by Bouthier (2008) as an example. It aims at approaching the physical techniques, the stages of a technological approach and the performance situations involved as scenarios and experience sharing. Here, we insist on the knowledge of the socio-technical systems of production and training.

This reflection about the use of the Code of Points echoes the debates on intervention. "In the field of sport, in the broad sense, an intervention corresponds to any professional act requiring skills, experience as well as theoretical knowledge to reach an objective, in various fields (schools, sports clubs, active leisure activities, rehabilitation, psychomotricity), for the benefit of various people, at a different age" (Association for Research in Intervention in Sport). It is not only a question about evaluation procedures, but also to understand the explicit and implicit consequences of a regulation. Besides, judging activity is also an important field.

The objective of this article is to contribute to a scientific debate on the controversies and also to present some data stemming from research in didactics. The idea is to highlight the very complex tasks of sport and physical education participants, giving them some theoretical and practical tools to better understand teaching and learning situations, to better analyse the practice of learners, and to propose new intervention procedures. We are interested in the first phase of the didactic transposition where the question of the social reference practice arises to set up practice, develop knowledge and school adaptations.

We believe that the regulations of sport are the first universal knowledge of sport as far as they are public, formalised, communicated and as far as they are the object of a social judgment which combine efficiency and utility registers (Robin, 1998). As such, the regulations can serve as references to teach novice athletes as well as more expert ones.

7.4 The rules of gymnastics: principles and originalities

Fundamentally in gymnastic and acrobatic activities, the regulations are used to assess performance, that is a feat, something exceptional, extraordinary, in a way, this means what can never be reached. For a long time, this high level of performance was symbolised by mark 10, without really knowing why. For a few years, no doubt, due to the weight of social developments, the regulations have changed, and as a result, there is no maximal mark set. Thanks to the rules, we can distinguish winners from losers and rank their performance. The role of regulations is to establish correct hierarchies because performances are objectively measured, due to the fact that the rules are respected by neutral and independent referees.

Moreover, the regulations guarantee the fundamental values of the sport in the Olympic movement: "equal opportunities with unequal results", "the symbolic victory always put back into play", "mutual respect for gymnasts and referees", etc. The regulations characterize the sports champion as an excellent social symbol.

The Code of Points aims at "coding the system of point allocation". It defines the parameters and the criteria which allow to differentiate the performances of gymnasts. These criteria are used to characterize "the conditions for victory". At the same time, the code of points also specifies "the conditions for judging", that is how the team of judges has to get organised and what the judges are allowed to evaluate. Thus, a certain number of objective and explicit data allow to give a certain mark.

The mark has to reflect exactly the level of performance of competitors. When considering the regulations published since 1936 (date of the first international Code of Points in gymnastics), it appears that the developers have always had a will to clarify permanently the assessment criteria to objectify them and to distinguish them.

7.4.1   1st originality

The regulations of gymnastics represent the first knowledge on the discipline (Robin, 1998). The contents are expressed, communicated, published, described, and they are subjected to social judgment. Indeed, in the context of acrobatic and gymnastic activities, the regulations are published in international journals which serve as references for judges and also as educational work for teachers. This is the first originality of acrobatic and gymnastic activities where the regulations are used as references for acrobats, coaches, judges, and spectators. The will to put this tool at the disposal of the different players to read gymnastics appeared explicitly in the intentions of the writers of the Code of Points at the International Federation of Gymnastics. "The current edition must be widely adopted as an indispensable reminder for every judge, coach, technician and gymnast" (Gander Arthur, President of the FIG from 1966 till 1976, Codes of checking GAM (clocking in GAM), 1979). Not all sport regulations do have this objective. However, it seems necessary to identify who

Gymnastics: a game of rules. 123

are the users to prepare the future adaptations. To do gymnastics, it is important to specify the different roles in the regulations.

7.4.2 2nd originality

Paradoxically, due to the developments on the technical level, the Code of Points did not refer to beginners any more. Indeed, the international Code of Points became an evaluation tool only for high performance gymnastics. Today, for a beginner it is not possible any more to do gymnastics with the same regulations as experts. For example, the technical elements ranked (organised into a hierarchy) integrate the most difficult skills performed at schools (such as somersaults) in the least valued categories. Frequent elements at school (such as the cartwheel or the round-off) do not score any point. The second originality of the regulations shows the necessary adaptation of the regulations to the levels of practice of gymnasts. To do gymnastics, it is essential to adapt the regulations to the requirements of school practice.

7.5 The essential rules of gymnastics

There are many different international code of points, often written by numerous national federations (FSGT, FSCF, UFOLEP, USEP, UNSS, etc.) and international federations (FIST, IMF, etc.). In principle, they are modified every new Olympic cycle. Since the first edition written by Lapallu, the regulations have gained in objectivity. The "codes" have classified and downgraded, categorised and ranked thousands of techniques. They have defined the "gymnastic silhouette", which is accepted by everyone. They have taken into account the technical innovations and apparatus developments. In some cases, rule changes even caused them. Finally, they have also caused international rivalries and balance of power. Generally speaking, this document changes quickly. Since it is questionable and modifiable, it is like a living organ.

However, permanent elements have structured the regulations in spite of constant changes. Essential characteristics appear which give rise to a diversity of small rules. In the wake of Deleplace (1983) and of Goirand (1990), the "main pillars" of the regulations are separated from the secondary rules. So, in gymnastics, there are three fundamental rules to evaluate performance in gymnastics.

7.5.1 The "difficulty" rule

The principle is the following one: "the more the gymnast presents difficult elements, the more points he/she scores". For example, according to the National Union of the School Sport (the French Federation for School Sport), at schools the gymnast has to do a round-off and a back handspring, but also a forward somersault to get the best mark in terms of difficulty. For gymnasts, the capacity to produce more acrobatics allows to have more chances of victory. This represents an additive logic. In fact, this requirement, which is specific to acrobatic activities, involves their physical (it can hurt) and psychological (it can frighten) integrity. Indeed, to get the best scores, gymnasts have to perform multiple complex airborne skills. So, they have "to take risks".

For half a century what has fundamentally changed is the construction of acrobatics, that is the multiplication of somersaults and twists. It is becoming more aerial, more upside down, more manual, etc. If this rule does not exist, then gymnastics would look like a sequence of simple movements and elementary forms, probably giving room for choreographic contents. It is a good scenario for tomorrow's schools. Gymnastics implies "encouraging the presentation of more complex acrobatics".

7.5.2 The "execution" rule

The principle is: "the more the performance of the gymnast is mastered, the more points he/she scores". For participants, the capacity to do gymnastics with ease and grace represents their technical control. Maintaining positions and balance, the amplitude of acrobatics, the quality of the body shapes, landing stability are relevant indicators to evaluate this aspect. This is what is meaningful in gymnastic aesthetics. Judges evaluate the degree of control. They verify whether what is presented is technically well executed and mastered. Every time a mistake is identified, it is penalized. Subtractive logic is used here. The judge subtracts points from a total score which is set in advance and which has considerable importance. So, gymnasts have "to control the risks taken". Technique favours this control. It is a question of doing something technically correct which implies doing something beautiful, doing something correct.

It is what is technically correct which is beautiful. This rule has not changed much over half a century. The quest for controlled movements is constant in this activity. The spirit of this rule aims at encouraging the safety of participants. If this rule doesn't exist, then acrobatic gymnastics would probably look like the games in an ancient circus where there would be higher acrobatic risks taken. It is also a scenario for tomorrow's schools. Therefore, gymnastics means "encouraging the control of complex acrobatics".

7.5.3 The "specific requirements" rule

The principle is "the more the gymnast moves in a rich and varied space, the more he/she scores points". The space being defined by the apparatus, the gymnast and the relationships from one to the other, the rule requires compulsory, specific transitions at every apparatus. For example, the gymnast has to cross both faces of the bar, and to perform an element on the bar and another one under the bar. The gymnast is urged to show the most diversified, the most aerial movements, etc. For participants, the capacity to exploit more and more the apparatus means more chances of victory. In this logic, points are added because the more the gymnast meets the requirements, the more points he gets. However, this rule also involves their physical and psychic integrities. They have "to take risks" to explore all the faces and all the levels of the apparatus.

This rule has evolved a lot for half a century. It leads to the co-ordination of more actions in all the planes of space. If this rule did not exist, then gymnastics would look like a sum of backward and forward movements on an apparatus in a few dimensions only. This was for instance the case when gymnastics was practised indoors and no longer outdoors in the 1930s. This rule also applies in the general or specialised practice of gymnastics. Indeed, it is not obligatory for the gymnast to perform on all the apparatus. There is a freedom of choice concerning the apparatus. The idea is close to the management of team sports where a player is asked to come into play, thus developing particular expertise in the game (here, the very rich exploitation of the space of an apparatus). This encourages new strategies and urges gymnasts to have more technical control. It is a good scenario for tomorrow's schools. Doing gymnastics implies "encouraging a variety of acrobatics in a still richer space" on apparatus which are strategically chosen by pupils and teachers.

7.6 The secondary rules of gymnastics

7.6.1 The "explicit" rules

The "secondary" rules correspond to the agreements which allow to decide between the best (for example, the male and female compulsory outfits, or also the bonuses). Among this set of data, four rules deserve attention because the consequences for pupils are important.

- First of all, it is necessary to specify "the play area". Gymnastics inevitably implies an apparatus with which the gymnast is confronted. The architecture of an apparatus is very important. For example, the latest developments of the vaulting horse contribute to a qualitative jump of the performances. According to the logic of the activity, it was necessary to make this apparatus even more aerial, more upside down, more manual. The vaulting table is the fruit of this challenge. It appeared for the first time in competition during the World Championships in Ghent (Belgium), in 2001. It is shorter (1.20m), wider (95cm), more tilted (7°), allows for more rebound, and it is better protected. From this perspective, the equipment is a didactic creation.

- The "performance duration" is a rule to be defined when necessary. But there is a contradiction: "When more technical elements are required, the less difficult they are"; which goes against the logic of the activity.

- The "number of players" is also an issue which needs to be defined. Theoretically, gymnastics is considered as an individual activity, but in reality gymnasts compete as a team. As we saw previously, team strategies are developed. However, school gymnastics can be done in teams (Amarouche & Nouillot, 1989). Synchronised or waterfall acrobatics are also possible ways. They existed in the history of gymnastics and even today they are used in some multi-sport federations or in new competition modes (gymnaestrada, euroteam, etc.).

- For floor gymnastics or on the beam, the "musical choices" can be useful to support choreography, synchronize the actions and facilitate indicators. Music is not a background sound. It is not a compulsory element. It is an additional constraint whose terms can be specified in order to be a real cultural project.

If the terms of the secondary rules are modified, this does not fundamentally distort the activity. But when motor activity is changed, these rules must be adapted to the characteristics of gymnasts and to the purposes of practice.

7.6.2 The "implicit" rules

The gymnastic and acrobatic activities have implicit rules which are recognised by all. For example, the rights of action on players are not legislated contrary to many sports activities. As a result, no rule forbids a competitor to strike his opponent, however no one would behave like that in competition. In the same way, gymnaestradas do not deliver either titles, or rankings, but they select the best sequences for a closing gala with the most acrobatic and the best performances. It is the same with the movements of gymnasts in the competition area, from the presentation of judges to the presentation of the different teams at the apparatus, from the silence and encouragements of spectators or the bowing of the gymnast to the panel of judges at the beginning and at the end of the performance: this is not written anywhere, but these regulations are tacitly and culturally accepted by gymnasts.

We deem necessary to update this implicit team regulations, particularly for beginners in order to facilitate the understanding of the spirit of gymnastics as well as the elaboration of the regulations by gymnasts. It should be noticed that gymnasts, physical education teachers or coaches underestimate the rules of gymnastics. However, pupils do little acrobatic gymnastics, which reproduces the traditional rules of static gymnastics and postures.

7.6.3 The judges' dynamics

In gymnastic and acrobatic activities, performance is assessed by judges. The evaluation is thus subjected to human judgment, the modalities are specified in the regulations. A mark is then the product of a negotiation (David, 2003) between judges for the sake of integrity, justice, and equity. The social activity of judges doing their work urged Durny (2011) to say that "the final mark is not a mere mean, but is the result a dynamics stemming from the mutual influence of judges and also from the competition context".

A system of constraints allows to guarantee the will of judges to respect equality between competitors since neutrality is utopian. The human dimension of judgment sometimes gives rise to excesses (such as cheating, coalition, pressure), but also points at the difficulty of the work of judges. To do gymnastics, it is thus necessary to allow gymnasts to go through the various social roles of the activity (as a gymnast, judge, coach, spectator) to understand the mechanisms and mistakes.

7.7 The contradiction arising from the regulations

The three essential rules which have been described, have fundamental consequences on motor activity in gymnastics. It is because of these rules, that gymnastic and also acrobatic motor activity exists. But all the logic of the activity results from the regulations. Thus the two rules, about "difficulty" and "specific requirements", urge gymnasts to take risks. They have to try more tricks and complex movements. However, the "execution" rule contributes to the control of the risks. Gymnasts have to control what they try. The regulations are thus right, because movements which would be either too dangerous, or not acrobatic enough are penalized.

A negative approach would be to limit performances to movements that either don't contain aerial phases, or to perform tricks leading to serious falls or injuries. Yet, this type of human activities exists, but does not belong to gymnastics. Thus gymnastics implies "managing" the contradiction between risk-taking which is inherent to the acrobatic activity and controling risks, which is necessary for the safety of gymnasts. This "contradictory unity" (Goirand, 1987) characterises the logic of this acrobatic activity as well as reveals its limits. According to the social role one has in gymnastics, the management of this essential contradiction will not be managed in the same way.

- In federal high performance gymnastics, the gymnast has no other choices than to learn more acrobatics and to try to master them during the competitions with his partners and against his opponents. He is particularly faced with a risk-taking logic.

- The judge has only one mission, that is to verify the control of performance, on D-day, at the right time. His point of view about the degree of skill is clear-cut. He can see the discrepancy between the requirements of the Code of Points and performance, respecting the logic of control of gymnastic techniques.

- The spectator appreciates what is "extraordinary and harmonious", that is what is magic (Jeu, 1977). Although he/she is mostly incompetent to judge the technique, he/she differentiates those who stay longer in the air and who turn fast. The spectator is also attracted by those who give an impression of ease and control. He/she is not there to pay attention to numerous failures and falls ... The spectator experiences emotions which are triggered by a logic of control and elegance.

- The coach is traditionally the one who decides on the best option: "to perform something difficult" or "to perform something well mastered". Contrary to the majority of sports activities, in gymnastics, the gymnast does not decides on the action to take, but the coach decides before the performance. We notice that the choices are often made in spite of adversity which is often underestimated by even the most successful coaches (Robin, 2011).

Thus, gymnastics is not to be considered as a traditional activity including the control of forms of technical bodies. It is a dynamic human activity which uses different strategies between various protagonists. This vitality exists only if the "risk-taking / control of the risk" contradiction of the regulations allows different possible choices.

7.8 The strategies of gymnasts and their coaches

However, in order to win, is it necessary to perform "more difficult" movements or to perform "more controlled" ones? - In fact, according to the distribution of points in the three sectors of the regulations, the strategies can be adapted. In gymnastics, today, the regulations are relatively balanced because according to the Code of Points, the values divide globally around 50% for the difficulty and the specific requirements and 50% for the control requirements. So, to win in gymnastics, there are three solutions:

1. The gymnast can perform more "difficult" movements than the others (i.e. he performs more acrobatics or does more complex acrobatics).

2. The gymnast can perform more "beautiful" movements than the others (i.e. he controls landing, position holding, attitudes and the postures). From this point of view, he develops a better adapted technique to the requirements of the activity.

3. The gymnast can perform more "difficult" and more "beautiful" movements than the others.

Therefore, such strategies are inferred by the regulations. The distribution of points is not made by chance; it produces the expected effects on the motor activity of gymnasts.

7.9 The rules of gymnastics as didactic variables

In learning situations, a didactic variable is the condition "which causes adaptations, regulations, changes in the strategies, when we act on it, and which finally allows to improve the notion which is being learnt" (Astolfi, 1990, p. 10). When certain rules of gymnastics are modified, both from the point of view of the principle of the rule or its value, then the motor activity of gymnasts is changed. So, the modification of the rule acts as a didactic variable. By acting on a parameter, we allow learners to progress. Therefore, it is necessary to identify which rule acts on which dimension of motor activity.

1. What is the consequence of an "over evaluation" of the "difficulty" rule? Giving this aspect of the mark more weight, would potentially encourage gymnasts to present more difficult technical elements. This sum of technical skills allows to evaluate quantitative progress. It requires the elaboration of a "common reference table", that is an inventory of the different techniques, their terminology and their value. This "over evaluation" can be useful when the teacher or the coach wishes to reward risk-taking in his pupils.

2. What is the consequences of an "over evaluation" of the "the execution" rule? Giving more weight to this aspect of the mark encourages pupils to control more the technical elements. This evaluation aims at qualitative progress. It is necessary to know the penalties and their value. This "over evaluation" can be useful when the teacher or the coach wishes to reward the requirements related to body control. Points could represent 75% of the result.

3. What is the consequence of an "over evaluation" of the rule of "specific requirements"? The richer the investigated space is, the better mark the gymnasts get. This evaluation aims at a qualitative progress. It requires to define the requirements

and their value. This "over evaluation" can be useful when the teacher or the coach wishes to give value to the movements in all the space of the apparatus. Points can represent up to 25% of the mark.

Understanding the rules of gymnastics as didactic variables is an approach, which in is in compliance with the rules that are more generally adopted in Physical Education (Boda & Récopé, 1991).

7.10 Conclusion

The objective of the rules of gymnastics is to allow gymnasts to perform better together. As in any sport, they are also used to rank gymnasts, maybe more than in the other activities. Finally, they aim at respecting the physical and psychological integrity of gymnasts. Therefore, it would be inappropriate not to know the regulations when this activity is taught at school.

For physical education teachers, the analysis of the Code of Points allows to understand the foundations, principles, values and uses. It enables to choose the strategies adapted to the objectives of training or education. So, if pupils want to become future "strategists-gymnasts", they have to understand the regulations of gymnastics and participate in their elaboration.

For educational purposes, the rules of gymnastics can be thought of as didactic variables. These variables indicate the variation possibilities, which are used by a teacher in the organization of learning conditions. Gymnastic and acrobatic activities offer pupils original technical skills. "Learning how to control one's body in space" requires gymnasts to know what the purpose is.

We believe that the study of the Code of Points as the foundations of gymnastic and acrobatic activities, is necessary to train and educate gymnasts, from beginner to expert. It requires a technological analysis with didactic purposes. An epistemology of the techniques is a relevant option to study scientifically the logical origin of techniques, their value, their impact and their meaning. Therefore, the Code of Points could be an object to scientific investigations.

References

Amarouche, P., & Nouillot, P. (1989). Objectif gym: vivre à l'heure des interclasses. In Editions du SNEP. *L'éducation physique et sportive, aujourd'hui ce qui s'enseigne* (pp. 101-104).

Astolfi, J. P. (1990). L'important, c'est l'obstacle. *Cahiers pédagogiques, 281*. Paris.

Boda, B., & Récopé, M. (1991). Instrument d'analyse et de traitement de l'APS à des fins d'enseignement. *Revue Éducation Physique. Sportive. 231*, 56-58.

Bouthier D. (2008). *L'approche technologique et la didactique professionnelle. Communication présentée lors de la 1ère rencontre suisse sur l'intervention en éducation physique et sport: Apport des courants de la recherche actuels pour la formation.* Lausanne: HEP Vaud.

David B., (2003). *Évaluation et notation en éducation physique et sportive. Regard sur la formation et perspectives de recherche.* Paris: INRP. Collection: documents, travaux, recherche.

Deleplace, R. (1983). La recherche sur la spécialisation, l'entraînement, la performance. In Editions Revue Sciences, Techniques, Activités Physiques et Sportives (STAPS). *La recherche en STAPS* (pp. 93-151). Nice 19-20 Sept. 1983.

Durny, A., (2011). Comment envisager la conception de programmes de formation des arbitres et juges à partir d'une analyse de leur activité effective. In F. Dosseville, & S. Laborde (Eds.), *Les différentes facettes de l'arbitrage*. Publibook.

Goirand, P. (1987). Une problématique complexe : des pratiques sociales des Activités Physiques et Sportives aux contenus d'enseignement en Education Physique et Sportive. In *Revue SPIRALES 1 complément* (pp 11-14). Eds UFR APS de Lyon.

Goirand, P. (1990). Didactique de la gymnastique et EPS. *Education Physique et didactique des Activités Physiques et Sportive*. Édition de l'Association des Enseignants d'Education Physique et Sportive (pp 74).

Goirand, P. (1994). Des pratiques sociales en gymnastique aux pratiques scolaires. *Revue SPIRALES 7*. Eds UFR APS de Lyon.

Goirand, P. (1996). Techniques sportives et culture scolaire. Éditions de la revue Education Physique. Sportive, 98-144.

Jeu, B. (1977). *Sport, émotion, espace*. Paris: Vigot.

Robin, J.-F. (1998). Transposition didactique : les savoirs de référence développés par quatre leaders de théories didactiques. In J.-F. Robin, & D. Hauw (Eds.), *Actualité de la recherche en EPS: bilan et perspectives* (pp. 109-118). Éditions Revue Education Physique. Sportive.

Robin, J.-F. (2011). Analyse des gestes professionnels des entraîneurs de l'équipe de France féminine de gymnastique lors de l'Olympiade 2004-2008. Actes du colloque de l'Association Recherche en intervention dans le Sport (ARIS).

CHAPTER 8

PORTRAITS OF HIGH PERFORMANCE RHYTHMIC GYMNASTICS IN BRAZIL - ANALYSIS AND PROPOSALS

Eliana de Toledo[1] & Kizzy Fernandes Antualpa[2]

[1] *UNICAMP - College of Applied Sciences (Brazil).*
[2] *University of São Paulo (Brazil).*

Correspondence to: eliana.toledo@fca.unicamp.br

8.1 Proloque

Before we start our appreciation of some portraits of high performance rhythmic gymnastics in Brazil, it is important that we characterize the scenario we are in.

We have been a part of the Brazilian rhythmic gymnastics history as we fulfilled the roles of athletes, coaches, and judges as well as members of federations, in and out of Brazil. For these reasons, our efforts in recent years were mainly in teaching at higher education institutions and knowledge production, aiming to address the demands in this historical process. In this context, we have chosen to carry out research and publish in the area just mentioned, understanding that there is still so much to be done for rhythmic gymnastics (RG) in this country.

Lectures in high performance RG in Brazil would be challenging, given the difficulty in finding research and data, and some issues are evident, as shown by different authors, judges, gymnasts and committees:

- The lack of continuous and well-founded public policies in sports, based on projects that actually meet the demands of the sport (and not to political interests, or electoral processes), as shown by Pinto (2008).

- The sport, and the professionals involved in it, still suffer from social prejudice mainly due to stereotypes attributed to high performance athletes, which can be historically understood by different reasons (Toledo, 2010). This is reflected, for instance, in the low wages paid for coaches as well as to professional athletes in this field, and their living conditions (benefits, conditions of work and training etc.).

- Despite the important role played by the internet, providing new specific materials about this modality, there are few suppliers of specialized equipment and clothing, for practice and training of this sport, due to the low number of participants (their products do not become attractive for sale in sports shops).

- A deficient infrastructure concerning training that might optimize athletes' potential, and the versatility of periodization (training plan) in order to achieve the performance of world-renowned teams.

- The small number of publications about high performance in rhythmic gymnastics in the country, with only a few books and articles.

- A limited body of poorly paid judges, which undermines domestic and international exchanges, and therefore an internal evaluation process more appropriate and consistent with international standards becomes a challenge. In this small group, only few have an international brevet, which reduces the possibilities for exchange of knowledge outside the country, as well as within the country (with the coaches, gymnasts, and judges).

- The poor qualifications of the coaches of the sport, either at the basic level (beginner), whether in high yield where the situation is worse.

Some of these problems are also experienced all around the world, in other countries in America (South, Central, North) but also in Europe, Asia and Africa; therefore, this study may bring enlightenment worldwide for high performance rhythmic gymnastics.

8.2 Portraits of past high performance rhythmic gymnastics in Brazil

The first high performance rhythmic gymnastics World Championship occurred in Budapest in 1963 (Bodo-Schmid, 1985). According to Velardi (1998) in the year of 1965 the first referee course for modern gym (as it was called in the past) took place, resulting in the establishment of a particular Code of Points, since RG differed from dance and artistic gymnastics (then called Olympic gymnastics). With the many changes that occurred over the years, RG started to found itself as a sport, looking for its identity in the field of sports gymnastics while being divided into two modalities - group and solo, where gymnasts could manipulate five devices for competition in: hoop, ball, rope, clubs, and ribbon.

In Brazil, the first records of RG were in 1953 and 1954, with the presentation of this modality in III and IV Technical Training Course and Teaching in Physical Education, organized and conducted by the Sports Department of the State of São Paulo (APEF, 1953). Even though this modality kept active through courses and demonstrations organized by different institutions, such as the Carioca Gymnastics Federation in 1968 (Saroa, 2005) and the Brazilian Sports Confederation (CBD) 1971, it was only in the 25th of November 1978 that the Brazilian Gymnastics Confederation (CBG) was founded.

The inclusion of solo RG in the Olympics Games (OG) officially occurred in 1984, in Los Angeles/USA (Bobo & Sierra, 1998). It was then that the first Brazilian RG gymnast, Rosane Flavilla, had a chance to participate with solo exercises, however failing to reach the finals. Thus, although we had little tradition and structure for

Portraits of high performance rhythmic gymnastics in Brazil. 141

this sport in the country, this invitation was a major milestone in the history of Brazilian high performance RG.

Table 8.1: Brazilian participation in Pan American Championships, World Championships and Olympic Games.

Competition	Place	Year	Modality	Rank	Observations
Pan American Games	Mar Del Plata (ARG)	1995	Group	3°	
Pan American Games	Winnipeg (CAN)	1999	Group	1°	
World Championship (Pre-Olympic)	Osaka (JPN)	1999	Group	8°	Qualified for the Olympics
			Individual	34°	
Olympic Games	Sidney (AUS)	2000	Group	8°	
Pan American Games	Santo Domingo (DOM)	2003	Group	1°	Qualified for the Olympics
World Championship (Pre-Olympic)	Budapest (HUN)	2003	Group	9° 1	
			Individual	27°	
Olympic Games	Athens (GRE)	2004	Group	8° 1	
Pan American Games	Rio de Janeiro (BRA)	2007	Group	1°	
World Championship (Pre-Olympic)	Patras (GRE)	2007	Group	11°	Qualified for the Olympics
			Individual	21°	
Olympic Games	Beijing (CHN)	2008	Group	12	
World Championship	Mie (JPN)	2009	Group	21°	
			Individual	29°	
World Championship	Moscow (RUS)	2010	Group	26°	Did not qualify for the Pre-Olympic
			Individual	22°	39 teams
Pan American Games	Guadalaraja (MEX)	2011	Group	1°	Did not qualify for the Olympics
			Individual	3°	General classification
Olympic Games	London (UK)	2012	Did not participate	---	---

Source: adapted from Antualpa (2011).

In the 1988 Olympics Games held in Seoul/Korea, Brazil failed to classify any gymnast. In 1992, at the OG in Barcelona/Spain, Brazil was represented by Marta Cristina Schönhorst, who qualified in 51st place in individual exercises (according to the gymnast own records). In 1996 at OG in Atlanta/USA, the International Federation of Gymnastics introduced group routines, opening new possibilities to compete in the sport and promoting its world-wide spread. But it was only in the 90s that Brazil started to have a more meaningful participation in international championships, achieving good rankings in South and Pan American Games (Antualpa, 2011).

Table 8.1 provides a brief background of Brazilian RG worldwide and highlights the participation of Brazilian gymnasts as individuals over group routines (with particular rankings), allowing the country to maintain a stable position with international significance. Therefore the largest investment of the Brazilian Gymnastics Confederation (CBG) is focused on group exercise, preparing, conducting and organizing the former team, as noted by current president of CBG, Luciene Resende, who expects the team to be "dedicated to training and able to represent the country in international competitions, in order to prepare for the World Championship, South America and Pan-American Games and 2016 Olympic Games, thereby generating new achievements for RG" (see www.cbginastica.org.br, accessed Feb / 2013).

8.3 Recent portraits of Brazilian high performance rhythmic gymnasts

In 2011, 23 state federations, with 219 affiliated entities (Schiavon et al, 2013), composed the Brazilian Gymnastics Federation (CBG). These entities are concentrated in the south and southeast regions of Brazil, which may be explained by different factors such as cultural, historical, and management. Regarding brazilian RG, the table 8.2 demonstrates a possible picture of how this sport is distributed on the national territory.

Concerning of the permanent team of 2012, it appears that twelve of the featured gymnasts are located mostly in the south of the country. The northeastern region appears with only one athlete composing the permanent individual team. The southeast region, that used to compose almost 90% of the national team, currently operates with

Portraits of high performance rhythmic gymnastics in Brazil. 143

only four gymnasts, all from Espírito Santo state (in the past, gymnasts belonged to São Paulo state). This table also shows the prevalence of some institutions composing the national team known by their respected work such as UNOPAR, Officer´s Club, School of Champions and Sadia.

Table 8.2: Summarized profile of selected gymnasts in 2012 and the "new team of 2013".

Gymnast	Modality	2012	2013	Club	State
Angélica Kvieczynski	Individual	Yes	Yes	Sadia	PR
Drielly Neves Daltoe -	Individual	Yes	No	Office´s Club	ES
Eliane Rosa Sampaio	Individual	Yes	Yes - Group	GNU	RS
Emanuelle Leal Lopes Lima*	Individual	Yes	Yes	Office´s Club	ES
Natalia Gaudio	Individual	Yes	Yes	School of Champions	ES
Rafaela Pedral Costa	Individual	Yes	Yes - Group	Arquidiocesano	SE
Amanda Pfleger	Group	Yes	No	Norsul	SC
Beatriz Pomini	Group	Yes	Yes	UNOPAR	PR
Bianca Mendonça	Group	Yes	Yes	UDESC	SC
Bruna Bialecki	Group	Yes	No	Agir	PR
Carolina Garcia	Group	Yes	No	School of Champions	ES
Dayane Amaral	Group	Yes	Yes	Agir	PR
Débora Falda	Group	Yes	Yes	UNOPAR	PR
Fabielle Cassol	Group	Yes	No	Agir	PR
Isabelle Andriotto	Group	Yes	No	UNOPAR	PR
Jéssica Sayonara Maier	Group	Yes	No	Guairacás	SC
Mayra Gmach	Group	Yes	Yes	Sadia	PR
Franciele Pereira	Group	No	Yes	Assomes	ES
Gabrielle Silva	Group	No	Yes	UNOPAR	PR
Gabriela Ribeiro	Group	No	Yes	GNU	RS
Isadora Silva	Group	No	Yes	UNOPAR	PR

At long last this is a representation of the scenario of the Brazilian RG high performance in 2012 and the new perspectives for 2013, looking forward to the new Olympic cycle (2013/2016) as a new team will be prepared for the 2016 Olympic Games (Rio de Janeiro - Brazil). Having their participation as a goal, a selection was held in March 2013 in order to constitute the "new" Brazilian national RG team (Table 8.2).

Regarding the "new" team composition, seven of the current gymnasts were already part of this group while the other four are new members, coming form states that had previous participation in the team. This shows a tendency for renovation, however with the maintenance of the work done in the states. It is possible to observe that among the gymnasts of the 2012 team, there was a migration from the individual team to the group team, allowing a reflection on the pursuit of career longevity of these athletes. Moreover, the table also presents the renewal of 36% of the team, enhancing the search for a strong group with specific characteristics for good performance to this Olympic cycle.

Despite the obvious search for renewal, it is noticeable the reinforcement of the team by the two entities that composed the framework in the previous year, indicating the maintenance of the previous work as well as it's philosophy and methodology, as shown by UNOPAR and GNU, indicating a possible lack of high-level gymnasts in other institutions and regions in this country. These data lead us to reflect about the need of a better structure for the formation and development of gymnasts, allowing the recycle of the national team with gymnasts from different regions, as well as advanced training for coaches. It is noteworthy that the geographic origin of these gymnasts that compose the national team may be explained by both cultural and historical aspects, but also by aspects related to sport management done by the states federations and CBG.

Most of the gymnasts come from the southern region of Brazil - states of Paraná, Santa Catarina and Rio Gande do Sul, which are historically known for their tradition in general gymnastics, once they hosted the first gymnastics association in the country, founded in 1867 SOGIPA - Gymnastics Society of Porto Alegre (Publio, 1998). In the last three decades the state of Paraná served as headquarters for the rhythmic gymnastics national team (on UNOPAR) and for the gymnasts that won international group championships, as well as hosted the CBG and a center of excellence in gymnastics (artistic and rhythmic) for over 15 years.

Other aspects were crucial to the spread and development of RG in the state of Paraná, and it was only possible thanks to the management of the federation of this state, through effective and organized planning, providing training courses for coaches, popularization festivals, and partnerships (with enterprises, the government and universities), among other actions (Stadnik, 2010). Then from the 90s the Espírito Santo state (Southeast) achieved greater prominence during the Olympic cycle 2005/2008 when the Brazilian team started to train together in this new house. So, with local gymnasts emerging on the national scenario and the group's coach Monika Queiroz living in the state, the CBG chose to transform the capital of this state (Vitória) in a center of excellence to house the national team. Finally the northeast region possesses a small place, but not less important in this scenario that might be justified by the CBG's newly investment in this region, which already had some outstanding gymnasts, and that housed the Brazilian individual team in the Olympic cycle 2005/2008. In 2006 this state received a training center funded by the government of the state of Sergipe in partnership with CBG as a way of valuing the achievements earned by gymnasts under the guidance of Maria Cristina Vital, that was coordinator of the RG committee of CBG and an international referee.

After these analyses it is important to initiate a reflection about the structure of the rhythmic gymnastics national championships, since they constitute the institutional spaces were the evaluation of the performance of the gymnasts can be done at the national level (and therefore provide a view to the future participation in international championships).

The Brazilian Gymnastics Federation is the institution responsible for "directing, disseminate, promote, organize and refine" gymnastics in all its possibilities (CBG, 2008, p.4), organizing events and championships. In the case of RG, the federation has the responsibility of promoting national championships at different levels such as the National Tournament, Brazil's Group's Cup and the National Championship.

8.3.1 National Tournament ("Torneio Nacional" - TN) – individual and group

The first edition of this national competition occurred in 2003, with rules adapted from the official Code of Points. In this tournament the gymnasts must submit two compositions to the judges: base categories (9/10 years old and 11/12 years old) must present one with hands-free and the other using one apparatus while junior (13/15 years old) and senior (above 16 years old) categories must use the apparatus in both composition. Groups also have adapted rules, with the requirement of only one composition (www.cbginastica.com.br, accessed April 2013).

This tournament covers beginner level athletes as well as those with higher technical skills, however they must have never participated in Brazilian championships. In 2012, the competition included the participants show in Table 8.3.

Table 8.3: Participants of the 2012 National Tournament (1st and 2nd phase).

	Groups	Level 1	Level 2
9/10 years old	8	27	133
11/12 years old	21	38	171
Junior	6	41	96
Senior	7	52	

Source: www.cbginastica.com.br, consulted in Feb/2013

For the 2013 tournament it was proposed that it should be held regionally, focusing initially on the five regions (North, Northeast, South, Southeast and Center-West) and later, according to the regulations stipulated by CBG (www.cbginastica.com.br, accessed in March 2013) athletes classified between the 1st and 4th place will be able to participate in the National Tournament. For group athletes there will be no restrictions, the only requirement is their participation in the regional tournaments by their geographic region.

In order to understand the importance of this tournament for the growth of the sport and allow us a brief analysis about the high performance RG´s national scene in each state we prepared Table 8.4.

Table 8.4 shows the participation of various regions of the country in this competition. It is noticeable that the South and Southeast regions are those who stand out on the national scenario, probably for their historical tradition, but also because of the capital accumulation and better infrastructure of these regions.

It is important to note the presence of three gymnasts (in emphasis), staring in the year of 2010, from states in the North and Northeast, confirming the aforementioned reflection on the importance of promoting the sport in the these regions by deploying the national training center in Aracaju (Sergipe State, northeast).

Table 8.4: Gymnasts champions of the National Tournament for the different categories 2008-2012.

YEAR	Step	PI– NII	PI – NI	INF – NII	INF– NI	Junior – NII	Junior- NI	Senior	CLUBS
2008	1ª	Ana Clara Deps – Oficiais (ES)	Hanely Bionot Leão - Unopar (PR)	Martina Caroline Stapenhorst - Mauá (SP)		Samyra Sumak de Melo – Oficiais (ES)		Vanessa Hagelmann - Joinville (SC)	Clube dos Oficiais da PMBM (ES)
	2ª	Angel Pereira Diniz – SERC (SP)		Gabrielle Moraes da Silva – Unopar (PR)		Dominique Rubensch – Sogipa (RS)		Vanessa Hagelmann – Joinville (SC)	SERC SANTA MARIA (SP)
2009	1ª	Nensar Vivian – AABB Tijuca (RJ)		Priscilla Carolina Dias Freitag – CIEF (DF)	Laura Reis Godoy – RGM (MG)	Juliana Keiko Campoira Kuroda – (PR)	Valéria Martini Montbach – AGIR (PR)	Ingrid Nerudha Vaz – RGM (MG)	AABB/TIJUCA - RJ
2010	1ª	---	Karoline Teixeira - Sadia (PR)		Laura Reis Godoy – GRM (MG)		Valéria Martini Montbach – AGIR (PR)	AMANDA CAMARGO – Espéria (SP)	CLUBE AGIR - PR
2011	2ª	Rafaela Silva - Sadia	Maiara Candido Monsul/SC	Keli'sa Tiba Rodrigues – CIEF/DF	Lara Porfirio Rebelo – Cief/DF		Rafaela Gehaske Sogipa	Luana Karle M. se Albuquerque – Coesi/SE	CLUBE AGIR - PR
2012	1ª	Amanda Regina Pivetta (Ass. Paulinense de GR/PR)	Geovanna Santos da Silva (Assomec-Clube dos Oficiais da PM/ES)	Karine Aparecida Walter (Ass. Rondonense de GR/PR)	Victória Kolbert Lima (Assomes/Clube dos Oficiais PM/ES)	Fernanda Filetti Ferreira (CETAF – ES)	Giovanna Fernandes Gorbea/BA	Natalia Nadine O. Silva (Ass. Ed. Esp. Cult. Tryade – SP)	ESCOLA MUNICIP AL HELENA KOLODY PR
	2ª				Luiza Bunaml Reverse Silva GRM (MG)		Vanessa Moreira Tavares (Nucleo Uniforde RG/CE)	Maria Yamaguchi (Pref.Mun. Cascavel/P R)	

Legend: Categories: PI – 9/10 years old; INF – 11/12 years old, Junior – 13/15 years old; Senior- above 16 years old. Levels: NI - Level I; NII - Level II.

Also regarding the National Tournament, Table 8.5 presents the group champions of the last editions of this competition. Note once again the strong presence of states from the South and Southeast regions in the first places.

Portraits of high performance rhythmic gymnastics in Brazil. 149

Table 8.5: Winners Groups of the National Tournament in different categories 2008-2012.

YEAR	STEP	9/10 years old	11/12 years old	JUNIOR	SENIOR
2008	1ª	CENTRO EDUCACIONAL VEM SER – CEVES (RN)	SOCIEDADE GINÁSTICA DE OGINVILLE (SC)	CLUBE DOS OFICIAIS DA PM/BM (ES)	CENEVES (RN)
	2ª	ASSOCIAÇÃO CURITIBANA DE GINÁSTICA RÍTMICA (PR)	SERC SANTA MARIA (SP)	CLUBE DOS OFICIAIS DA POLÍCIA MILITAR (ES)	SOCIEDADE GINÁSTICA DE OGINVILLE (SC)
2009	1ª	CLUBE AGIR (PR)	COLÉGIO ÁBACO (SP)	CENEVES (RN)	CLUBE ESPORTIVO INTERGADO
	2ª	ASSOCIAÇÃO GINÁSTICA POLINE IGLESIAS (GAPI) (PR)	CETAF (ES)	ASSOCIAÇÃO GINÁSTICA POLINE IGLESIAS (GAPI) (PR)	ADIEE / UDESC (SC)
2010		CLUBE AGIR - PR	Clube AGIR/PR	SOCIEDADE DE GIN DE OGINVILLE - SC	CEGAM/ES
2011		CLUBE AGIR – PR	ESCOLA MUNICIPAL HELENA KOLODY – PR	COLEGIO ÁBACO – SP	ASS. EDUCACIONAL ESP. CULTURAL TRYADE – SP
2012		ESCOLA MUNICIPAL HELENA KOLODY/PR	ESCOLA MUNICIPAL HELENA KOLODY - PR	ASS. EDU. ESP CULTURAL TRYADE - SP	ASS. EDU. ESP, CULTURAL TRYADE - SP

An interesting analysis of these two tables (8.4 and 8.5) is the diversity of institutional profiles that are promoting RG and are participating in this type of event. The presence of clubs in competitive events is a recognized fact in literature, despite the decline of these institutions that have been suffering from a lack of funding (Gallati, 2012). On the other hand, it is possible to observe in Table 8.5 the presence of schools (private and public), associations and other institutions of culture, education and / or sports promoting the RG in different states. These data are encouraging and make reference to Paes's research (2012, 2007) by stating the correlation between the widespread of this practice (democratization), the growing number of practitioners and the evolution in the sport (up to top performance).

Table 8.6: Participants of the Brazilian National Group's Championship - 2011/2012.

Categories	Groups numbers		Gymnasts number		Champions	
	2011	2012	2011	2012	2011	2012
9/10 years	2	2	12	12	AGIR (PR)	AGIR (PR)
11/12 years	7	7	42	42	AGIR (PR)	UNOPAR (PR)
Junior	9	10	54	60	UNOPAR (PR)	SADIA (PR)
Senior	7	7	42	42	Clube dos Oficiais (ES)	Clube dos Oficiais (ES)
Total participants: of	25	26	150	156		

In the case of RG we believe that the diversity of institutions is probably due to the formation of coaches and teachers who work in them (especially in schools), because we hardly hear or read reports that indicate that this offer is actually an institutional desire (by the club members; school and sports leaders - public or private, etc.).

8.3.2 Brazil Group's Cup and Brazilian National Group's Championship (Ilona Peuker)

These competitions are organized especially for the group program. The Brazil Group's Cup suggests that teams participate with two different compositions, according to the apparatus required in the current cycle, and as the National Tournament this competition allows the participation of any entity affiliated or not to a federation, and there is still a flexible code (rules).

Concerning the Brazilian National Group's Championship - Ilona Peuker, is an event characterized as an official competition that requires the presentation of two compositions without adjustments in regulation based on the current apparatus of the Olympic cycle, following the FIG's Code of Points. Table 8.6 presents data about this league in recent years (most of them obtained from the CBG website - www.cbginastica.com.br).

Table 8.6 presents other indications of the Brazilian RG's scenario. Comparing the total number of participants for this event we realized that there was the addition of a group from 2011 to 2012, and therefore, an increase of 6 gymnasts in the same period, which is negligible for the sport. In this same line of reasoning, it was observed that the number of gymnasts and the number of groups by category remained almost the same from one year to the other indicating that there has been a replacement of gymnasts in the participating institutions.

The situation can also be explained because the same gymnasts participated in this same competition for two years, staying in the same category for those years as in the base categories (9/10 and 11/12 years). Although there was no significant increase in participants, there seems to be a constant recycling of athletes, since base categories are not decreasing. Therefore we might see the presence of the same institutions in the competition, and almost no changes in the Champions event that come mostly from the same institutions, especially in the 9/10 years and senior category. These are the institutions that have supplied consistently the gymnasts that make up the Brazilian team today.

Regarding the quantity these are a very low numbers considering the size of our country, the number of population and the large amount of existing clubs in it. But besides this we are also concerned about the ways rhythmic gymnastic will be developed and offered in physical education classes at school (Toledo, 2009; Schiavon & Nista-Piccolo, 2007), in the public programs and projects, as a physical activity or high performance method, and especially how it will be encouraged by the state federations, and also by the CBG's management policy, specially at a time where the Artistic Gymnastics comes to stand out.

Regarding the quality of the work presented in these championships, it is worth mentioning Lourenço's research (2012) which along with other researchers analyzed the variation of choreography structure and types of apparatus's throws in group choreography in t championships for junior and senior categories. These studies reinforce the need for change in the work of these institutions and propose different techniques for working with groups, because in spite of the difference in educational lines we found the compositions, choreography structure, transitions and apparatus's throws (together) in this championship of little. However, the winner groups have a lot of creativity and gymnasts have been achieving the technical level of international champion teams.

8.3.3 Brazilian National Individual's Championship

Like the National Group's event this championship is recognized by CBG as an official competition and one that selects the future representatives of the country in international events. In this context, the standards of organization the FIG for junior and senior categories, and the Pan American Union of Gymnastics (UPAG) for basic categories are followed.

In these events the gymnasts must present four different compositions, with four different apparatus diverging from the adapted regulation to competitions like the National Tournament that only works with two apparatus by category. The Table 8.7 suggests a panorama of high performance rhythmic gymnastics in Brazil and shows the number of gymnasts participating in the event, as well the gymnasts and champion's teams in 2011 and 2012.

Portraits of high performance rhythmic gymnastics in Brazil. 153

Table 8.7: Participants of the Brazilian National Individual´s Championship - 2011/2012.

	Gymnasts number		Gymnasts Champions		Champion´s Teams	
	2011	2012	2011	2012	2011	2012
9/10 years	38	18	Mariany Myiamoto - Soc. Ginástica OGinville (SC)	Geane Costa - Sadia (PR)	Sadia (PR)	Sadia (PR)
11/12 years	60	48	Mayra Siñeriz - Clube dos Oficiais (ES)	Barbara Domingos - Clube Agir (PR)	AGIR (PR)	AGIR (PR)
Junior (12/13 years)	45	47	Emanuelle Lima - Clube dos Oficiais da (ES)	Mayra Siñeriz - Clube dos Oficiais (ES)	Sadia (PR)	GNU (RS)
Junior (14/15 years)				Andressa Jardim - GNU (RS)		
Senior	45	36	Natalia Gaudio – Escola de Campeãs (ES)	Natalia Gaudio – Escola de Campeãs (ES)	Sadia (PR)	Sadia (PR)

The Brazilian Championship (BC) is clearly a competition that combines a smaller number of participants compared to the National Tournament which brings between 200 and 300 participants per event (see Table 8.4). This fact is justified by the official code of points that demand the gymnasts to present four individual series and two groups' choreographies. Besides this difference is the Brazilian Championship that pre selects the gymnasts who will compose the national teams.

8.4 Analyzing a mosaic of portraits

Note that the competitions organized by CBG (nationally) have different formats and goals, while the National Tournament and Brazil group's Cup aims the democratization the sport, as the Brazilian National Championship (individual and group) seek to identify the best gymnasts in the country and select them for participation in international events. However, it is worth noting that the base championships (NT and Brazil group's Cup) are considered as "stepping stones" for the bigger teams. From a research document on the website of the CBG (www.cbginastica.com.br, accessed March 2013) we can identify that the great names of Brazilian RG nowadays have attended these tournaments: Mayra Sineriz – Clube dos Oficiais (ES) - 2nd place – 9/10 years (2008); Rafaela Pedral Costa - Coesi (SE) - 4th placed -Senior (2008); Bárbara de Kassis Domingos – AGIR (PR) - 1st place 9/10 years (2009).

These data corroborate the existence of these events as motivators and constituents of a gymnast's training for high performance, which together with other events promoted regionally by each state Federation (massification and officials) are responsible for the process of improving the achievement of gymnasts in the high performance.

Antualpa (2011) found that teams that lead the ranking in these official championships are part of RG's training centers (of excellence) in the country. The research encompassed three centers, two of them in the south and one in the northeast region. The first, based in Londrina (PR), is a university - University of Northern Parana (UNOPAR). The second training center was funded by Sadia Group / City of Toledo / SESI and is located in Toledo (PR). And the third national training center, located in Aracaju (SE) is the headquarters of the Brazilian national group, with the support of the Brazilian Gymnastics Federation (CBG). It was found that there are similarities and differences between those centers. As for the similarities observed: a) specific and unique structure for rhythmic gymnastics practice, which does not compromise the specificity of training arising from adjustments of space for other activities; b) official platform and viable height for the practice, providing security and adaptation to international standards; c) ballet bar and mirrors, providing technical training; d) stockroom for all materials used in the practice (official and patronage, individual and group); e) a coach responsible and the assistance of a coordinator for the development and implementation of planning; f) selection process of talent, in order to bring new gymnasts to the teams. In the case of the Brazilian team, this step is performed with the goal of creating a team of senior category.

Regarding the differences, it was found that: a) there is a variation in the number of official platforms in each center (UNOPAR - 1, Sadia / Toledo / SESI - 3, CNT - 2); b) presence of bleachers for public visitation, except in UNOPAR where this structure is built in the gymnasium (auxiliary); c) specific room to ballet practice with necessary equipment in only one of the centers; d) expert professionals for ballet classes in just two training centers, and finally e) a division of general and specific physical preparation in only a training center. Further issues concerning the periodization of training conducted by these teams were analyzed in the research but will not be addressed in this text.

8.5 Possibilities of new portraits

Looking at some of the portraits of high performance RG's in Brazil it is possible to conclude that they were constituted in two moments, the first being a few years ago (only 70 years) and the second of recent history, about 20 years, with medals and standout places in the international scenario, especially in the group's program. Changes in the many factors related to the development of Brazilian gymnastics in general are required, as well in rhythmic gymnastic. In concern to the general aspects of gymnastics, we refer to the study of Cruz, Paoliello and Toledo (2010) about the role of universities, the media, the CBG and federations, among others. Regarding the aspects that affect specifically RG's development, previously analyzed data and others arising from a broader scenario, such as from the participation in events, courses, meetings with officials, among others, allows us to present the some issues and the possibilities for overcoming them:

- There is still an insufficient number of training centers, given the size of the Brazilian territory, and the offer of the sport in different states. Thus, this increase is necessary and can be taken at first with a center by region (and there may be more than one per region, depending on the results already obtained by each state in the same region).

- There is a lack of investment in training technicians, as well as in organizing judges courses, or exchanges (national and international), which could be promoted by CBG and also by universities (alone or in partnership).

- Not all physical education courses in the country include rhythmic gymnastics as a content of gymnastics' discipline. Thus, it is necessary that we have a greater investment in the formation of these professionals, comprehending the rhythmic gymnastics in curriculum, both in teaching and in high performance.

- There should be an increase in the input of rhythmic gymnastics in the school's physical education curriculum, providing access to a greater number of people, since it is shown by this research that little of the sport is present in the context of schools.

- Better structuring of RG's massification events in many states and at the national level (diversification of difficulty levels, local and regional phases with better infrastructure, various forms of awards and classification etc.), motivating greater participation of the gymnasts (beginners, intermediate, and training), especially considering that athletes comes from different contexts (schools, clubs, associations, university extension projects).

Portraits of high performance rhythmic gymnastics in Brazil. 157

- The creation of more and better opportunities for dialogue between experts and researchers to exchange knowledge, which may enhance RG's high performance.

Finally, in order to achieve greater development of high performance RG's we can benefit from the international experience, using current experiences as a database of ideas for future reflection, reconstruction and execution.

In this way, we can take advantage from these national's portraits, identifying their problems and trying to outline some solutions from scientific studies as well as from the experiences of other countries. There are a variety of possibilities in Cuba (role of government of shaping the sport and creating training centers), in Eastern European countries, Australia and Japan (in training programs, as pointed out by Nunomura, 2001), and in the program "FIG Academy", which seeks to bring the different countries a new framework of knowledge for the development of high performance gymnastics (three technical levels, addressed to beginners and experienced technicians).[1]

Although this scenario seems apparently not favorable for RG's development, that there are some successful initiatives different in regions of Brazil that should be followed alongside with what has been developed by other countries. They are:

- The creation of a graduate course in rhythmic gymnastics proposed by UNOPAR. Besides the capacitating coaches and teach-

---
[1] Currently in Brazil there are eight coaches (previously invited by CBG) who have the complete formation of the FIG Academy and should be responsible and influenced to disseminate this knowledge. However the current situation of vocational training is still facing improvement initiatives for both professionals initiation and for those who work with the high level. Training courses and expansion of knowledge that should be offered by the state federations, and especially by CBG are offered mostly by groups and entities with specific goals.

ers, allowing them to follow the practice of excellence teams, this institution also contributes with knowledge production.

- The establishment of a public-private partnership as the case of one of the best teams in the country that has been created about three years ago involving the Department of Sports of the Municipality (government), the company Sadia (private sector) and SESI - Social Service for Industry (autarchy). This partnership is an example for the promotion of high performance sports.

- Organized to expand the gymnastics reach, a basic level event such as the Troféu São Paulo (State of São Paulo) has been created. Although it can still be improved in its structure, it has an interesting model. Divided in categories (4), levels of complexity for each of these categories (5 - A, B, C, D and E) and free choreographies, it allows the gymnasts to be evaluated twice a year, passing from a low to a higher level each time.

- The academic event SIGARC - International Symposium on Artistic and Rhythmic Gymnastics Competition, which is organized biannually by the State Universities of São Paulo (UNICAMP, UNESP, and USP), with public and private partners, and is currently in its 3rd. edition. In this event there are several discussion panels, workshops, meetings, and a poster session on the high performance rhythmic gymnastics, establishing itself as the only event in the country that promotes and produces knowledge in this area (with national and international authors).[2]

---

[2] The proceedings of SIGARC (abstracts in English and Spanish) can be found under www.gimnica.com.

- Increasing the production of knowledge on the subject, which although still shy, shows up as a breakthrough at the national level in books, articles, monographs, theses, and dissertations.

- The existence of some specific web sites about gymnastics with technical information (events, links to associations, etc.) and academic (texts, articles, scientific meetings, etc.), contributing to the training of professional and the dissemination of the sport in the country. Examples are www.ginasticas.com and www.gimnica.com.

And to close this text, we could not fail to mention that rhythmic gymnastics and other sports that achieve high performance develops themselves thanks to the professionals who are behind these actions. In other words, there are people interested in the growth of the sport, dedicated, but mostly humble, and who are willing to grow collectively, aware that the sharing of knowledge and the sum of efforts is an excellent way to reach greater goals.

References

Antualpa, K. F., & Paes, R. R. (2013). Structure of rhythmic gymnastics training centers in Brazil. *Science of Gymnastics Journal, 5*(1), 71–79.

Antualpa, K. F. (2011). *Centros de treinamento de ginástica rítmica no Brasil: estrutura e programas.* (Master's thesis). Faculdade de Educação Física, Universidade Estadual de Campinas, Campinas.

APEF (1953). *Revista da Associação de professores de Educação Física, 1*(1). São Paulo: Associação de Professores de Educação Física, Location.

Barbosa-Rinaldi, I. P., & Souza, E. P. M. (2008). Saberes ginásticos necessários à formação profissional em educação física: encaminhamentos para uma estruturação curricular. *Revista Brasileira de Ciências do Esporte, 29*, 227-243.

Bernardes, G. (2010). Revivendo o meu encontro com a ginástica rítmica. In E. Paoliello, & E. de Toledo (Eds.), *Possibilidades da ginástica rítmica* (pp. 45-71). São Paulo: Phorte.

Bobo, M., & Sierra, E. (1998). *Ximnasia Rítmica Deportiva - Adestramento e competición*. Santiago de Compostela: Lea.

Bodo Schmidt, A. (1985). *Gimnasia Ritmica Deportiva*. Barcelona: Hispano Européia.

Brazilian Gymnastics Federation (CBG). Available at: `http://www.cbginastica.com.br/web/`.

Cruz, B. C., Paoliello, E., & de Toledo, E. (2010). A divulgação da Ginástica Geral: Identificação de uma problemática a partir de um estudo de caso. *CONEXÕES – Revista da Faculdade de Educação Física da UNICAMP, 10* 10-27.

De Rose Jr., D. (2002). A criança, o jovem e a competição esportiva: considerações gerais. In D. de Rose Jr. (Ed.), *Esporte e atividade física na infância e na adolescência: uma abordagem multidisciplinar* (pp. 67-76). Porto Alegre: Artmed.

Fédération Internationale de Gymnastique (FIG). Available at: `http://www.figgymnastics.com/index2.jsp?menu=diswag`. Last access in February 2013.

Filin, V. P., & Volkov, V.M. (1998). *Seleção de talentos nos desportos*. Londrina: Midiograf.

Laffranchi, B. (2005). *Planejamento, aplicação e controle da preparação técnica da ginástica rítmica: análise do rendimento técnico alcançado nas temporadas de competição*. (Doctoral dissertation). Faculdade de Ciências do Desporto e de Educação Física, Universidade do Porto, Porto.

Laffranchi, B. (2001). *Treinamento desportivo aplicado à ginástica rítmica*. Londrina: Unopar Editora.

Lebre, E. (1993). *Comparativo das exigências técnicas e morfológicas em Ginástica Rítmica Desportiva*. (Doctoral dissertation). Faculdade de Ciências do Desporto e de Educação Física da Universidade do Porto, Porto.

Lourenço, M. R. A., & Chagas, F. (2012). Análise das formações nos grupos da categoria adulto participantes do campeonato brasileiro de ginástica rítmica de 2011. In L. Schiavon (Ed.), *Caderno de Resumos do III Seminário Internacional de Ginástica Artística e Rítmica de competição - SIGARC* (pp. 44-52). Rio Claro: UNESP.

Monteiro, S. (2000). *Quantificação e classificação de cargas de treino em ginástica rítmica: estudo de caso – preparação para o campeonato do mundo de Osaka 1999 da seleção nacional de conjunto Senior*. (Master's thesis). Faculdade de Ciências do Desporto e de Educação Física, Univeridade do Porto, Porto.

Nunomura, M. (2001). *Técnico de ginástica artística: uma proposta para a formação profissional*. (Doctoral dissertation). Faculdade de Educação Física, Universidade Estadual de Campinas, Campinas-SP.

Paes, R. R., & Galatti, L. R. (2012). Pedagogia do Esporte: o clube sócio-esportivo como uma nova possibilidade de ambiente. In G. Tani et al. (Eds.), *Celebrar e Lusofonia: Ensaios e Estudos em Desporto e Educação Física* (pp. 421-442). Belo Horizonte: Casa da educação física.

Paes, R. R. et al. (2007). *Pedagogia do esporte e iniciação esportivas infantil: as relações entre dirigente, família e técnico*. In A. A. Machado (Eds.), *Especialização Esportiva Precoce - Perspectivas Atuais da Psicologia do Esporte* (pp. 23-56). Jundiaí: Fontoura.

Pinto, L. M. S. M. (2008). *Políticas Públicas de Lazer no Brasil: uma história a contar*. In N. C. Marcellino (Ed.), *Políticas Públicas de Lazer* (pp. 79-96). Campinas: Alínea.

Publio, N. S. (1998). *Evolução histórica da ginástica olímpica*. Guarulhos: Phorte.

Santos, J. C. E., & Santos, N. G. M. (1999). *História da Ginástica Geral no Brasil*. Rio de Janeiro: JCE dos Santos.

Sarôa, G. R. (2005). *A história da ginástica rítmica em Campinas. 2005*. (Master's thesis). Faculdade de Educação Física, Universidade Estadual de Campinas, Campinas.

Schiavon, L. M. (2009). *Ginástica artística e história oral: a formação desportiva de ginastas brasileiras participantes de jogos Olímpicos (1980-2004)*. (Doctoral dissertation). Faculdade de Educação Física, Universidade Estadual de Campinas, Campinas.

Schiavon, L. M., & Nista-Piccolo, V. L. (2007). A ginástica vai à escola. *Movimento – Revista da Faculdade de Educação Física da UFRS, 13*(3), 131-150.

Schiavon, L. M. et al. (2013). Panorama da Ginástica artística feminina brasileira de alto rendimento esportivo: progressão, realidade e necessidades. *Revista Brasileira de Educação Fisica e Esporte da USP, 27*(3), 423-436.

Stadnik, A. M. V. (2010). Um panorama da ginástica rítmica no Paraná. In E. Paoliello, & de Toledo, E. (Eds.), *Possibilidades da ginástica rítmica* (pp. 237-267). São Paulo: Phorte.

Toledo, E. (2009). A ginástica rítmica e artística no ensino fundamental: uma prática possível e enriquecedora. In E. C. Moreira (Ed.), *Educação Física Escolar - desafios e propostas I* (2nd ed., pp. 127-156). Jundiaí: Fontoura.

Toledo, E. (2010). *A legitimação da ginástica de academia na modernidade: um estudo da década de 80*. (Doctoral dissertation). São Paulo: Pontifícia Universidade Católica de São Paulo.

Toledo, E., & Silva, P. C. C. (Eds.) (2013). *Democratizando o ensino da Ginástica – estudos e exemplos de sua implantação em diferentes contextos sociais.* Várzea Paulista: Fontoura.

Vaeyens, R. et al. (2008). Talent identification and development programmes in sport: current models and future directions. *Sports Medicine, 38*(9), 703-714.

Velardi, M. (1998). Ginástica Rítmica: a necessidade de novos modelos pedagógicos. In V. L. Nista-Piccolo (Ed.), *Pedagogia dos Esportes.* Campinas: Papirus.

CHAPTER 9

GYMNASTICS COACHING AND SCIENCE: BIOMECHANICS PERSPECTIVES

Gareth Irwin, Geneviève K. R. Williams & David G. Kerwin

Cardiff Metropolitan University - Cardiff School of Sport (United Kingdom).
Correspondence to: girwin@cardiffmet.ac.uk

9.1 Introduction

This chapter aims to demonstrate how biomechanics can contribute to the effectiveness of the coaching process. Through the application of mechanical principles to biological systems biomechanics provides a relevant scientific tool. This chapter leads the reader through specific examples of how knowledge of biomechanics can assist the coach in the gym through the development of tacit knowledge in relation to how skills 'work' and how best to develop skills. This chapter explores key research themes applied to the sport of gymnastics, specifically the coaching biomechanics interface (Irwin et al., 2013), the evolution of complex skills (Irwin et al., 2011; Kerwin & Irwin, 2011) and how the changes in apparatus and code of points have influenced the development of skills, with examples drawn from the research presented on the female Tkatchev by Kerwin and Irwin (2010; 2011) and Irwin et al. (2011). Fundamental to gymnastics skill learning is the development of techniques that are effective, efficient and safe. Research has identified how coaches develop skills from a psychological and conceptual perspective (Irwin et al., 2005), combined the principles of training and biomechanics to the increase the understanding of the most effective skill pathways for learning gymnastics movements (Irwin & Kerwin, 2005, 2007a, 2007b). Contemporary theories of motor control have been embedded into how best to develop skills. Research by Williams et al. (2012), will be discussed with reference to recent motor learning literature.

9.2 Coaching biomechanics interface

The coaching biomechanics interface is a term that aligns itself with the central mission of the International Society of Biomechanics in

Sport: it aims to facilitate the application of theory into practice within coaching and sporting performance. The coaching biomechanics interface goes one step further and explains how scientific knowledge, based on the universal laws of biology and mechanics, can be used in combination with the tacit knowledge inherent to coaches (Irwin et al., 2004). This symbiotic relationship drives the development of meaningful information that is both scientifically sound and coaching relevant. This information can help a coach to give relevant feedback to performers, whilst the science can be used to develop technologies; all in the interests of improving athletic performance. The coaching biomechanics interface then aims to make training effective, efficient and safe for the development of training drills, strength and conditioning programmes and skill learning (Irwin et al., 2013). The cyclical process develops coaching knowledge and understanding of skill development, therefore enhancing the overall education of the sport. The concept of the "coaching biomechanics interface" is further developed by the model of progression development presented in Irwin et al. (2005). This model explains how coaches develop a conceptual understanding of skill and skill development based on four themes (current knowledge, coaching resources, a mental image and biomechanical description of the final skill). This conceptual understanding allows coaches to understand the key phases and timings of the skills they are developing. In addition it facilitates the development of progressions through the replication of the spatial and temporal characteristics of the target skill. The development of skills forms the central focus.

9.3 Complex skills analysis

The measurement of gymnastics performance is based on the code of points, a system that quantifies gymnastic performance based on a judge's score. The code of points (COP) changes every four years, with updates based on formal regulations throughout the year. The COP provides an ever-evolving system in gymnastics assessment. In recent years changes in apparatus have taken place, such as the removal of the horse and introduction of the vaulting table, and the change in dimensions of bar separation in female uneven bars. As well as the removal of 10 score, and a more open ended judging system was introduced in 2004. The Tkatchev provides a good example of how biomechanics has contributed to the evolution of gymnastics skills. This release and re-grasp skill was introduced into artistic gymnastics by Soviet biomechanist and methodologist Smovevski in 1969. It was first performed in the late1970's in men's gymnastics (Alexander Tkatchev) and in the 1980's by female gymnasts (Nissenen, 1985). For both men and women the Tkatchev has evolved into an essential skill for the attainment of high difficulty scores on the high and uneven bars. Altering the body position in the flight phase increases difficulty (FIG, 2012). Women most commonly perform this skill in either a straddle or piked body position. In addition, men also perform the Tkatchev in a straight body position, also adding twists. Since the 1996 Olympics the Tkatchev skill became more popular in female gymnastics due to an increase in the inter bar distance from 1.6 m to 1.8 m. This allowed females to swing more freely and performed more complex version similar to their male counterparts. Different versions are defined by shape in the flight phase, and swinging direction relative to the low bar (outward or inward)

Gymnastics coaching and science: biomechanics perspectives. 167

Figure 9.1: Left = Outwards facing Tkatchev, Middle = Inward facing Tkatchev and Right = Toe-on Tkatchev (adapted from Irwin et al., 2011).

has also become an option (Irwin et al., 2011). Kerwin and Irwin (2010) compared the outward and inward variants of the women's straddle Tkatchev to investigate the influence of the different techniques on the musculoskeletal demands of the skill. More recently, with the emergence of a the Toe-on Tkatchev new questions have been raised. Specifically can newer variants provide more opportunity for women to create the release characteristics needed to perform the straight Tkatchev?

Biomechanical research has shown that for the outward, inward and toe-on version of the Tkatchev there was a greater angle of release for the Toe-on version, as the gymnast extends the hip joint to reach the release point (Irwin et al., 2011; Kerwin & Irwin, 2011; Figure 9.1). The Toe-on Tkatchev on uneven bars therefore appears to be an advancement of the inward variant of this skill, enabling the gymnasts to increase key release variables (Table 9.1). Particularly vertical velocity, (and hence flight time) and angular momentum were increased. As such, body shape in the flight phase can be changed to the point where straight Tkatchevs are beginning to appear following Toe-on Tkatchevs in women's competitions. Based on the results of the study, coaches should consider the dominant role of the hips in developing specific release characteristics.

Table 9.1: Mean [±SD] release parameters for the Toe-on straddle Tkatchev on uneven bars (adapted from Irwin et al., 2011)

	Outward	Inward	Toe on
T_{flight} [s]	0.51 ± 0.07	0.54 ± 0.08	0.60 ± 0.06
Φ [°]	38 ± 14	58 ± 7	66 ± 6
v_y [m/s]	−2.04 ± 0.15	−2.05 ± 0.25	−1.71 ± 0.10
v_z [m/s]	1.42 ± 0.60	1.71 ± 0.53	1.95 ± 0.48
L_n [SS/s]	−0.19 ± 0.06	−0.32 ± 0.04	−0.37 ± 0.11

The musculoskeletal differences were also examined. Table 9.2 highlights the difference in the shoulder work with the outward (old) version of the Tkatchev being requiring an opposite action at the shoulder compared to the inward and toe-on version. During the inward and toe-on version the gymnast is actively opening their shoulder joint; this is desirable information for coaches. The current study provides an example of how the coaching biomechanics interface can use scientifically grounded data from an ecologically valid setting to inform technique development.

Table 9.2: Percentage Hip (H) and Shoulder (S) Work for Outward (Outw.), Inward (Inw.) and Toe-On straddle Tkatchev on uneven bars.

	Outw.	Inw.	Toe on	Outw.	Inw.	Toe on
Joint Work	H	H	H	S	S	S
Positive	90%	80%	90%	70%	35%	30%
Negative	10%	20%	10%	30%	65%	70%

Developing skills and optimizing the performance of those skills is a key element of the coaching biomechanics interface. Skill learning is an area underpinned by both biomechanics and motor learning theory.

9.4 Skill development and learning

Motor skill learning and development is fundamental to performance in sport. The aim of learning is to optimally satisfy the technical and therefore biomechanical demands of a task within the constraints imposed by the environment (apparatus) and the body (gymnast) (Newell et al., 1986). As discussed previously, a coach and a performer often develop a mind set of what a skill should look like. This mind set is based on a conceptual understanding of how the skill should be performed, watching experts execute the skill, and an understanding if the biomechanics of the skill (Irwin et al., 2005).

Knowledge of how technique changes as we learn and develop towards a more successful technique is fundamental in coaching, in order that we can effectively guide learners to a better performance outcome. Research and anecdotal evidence suggest that novice's techniques are likely to be characterised by some common movement pattern characteristics (Bernstein, 1967; Busquets et al., 2011; Newell, 1986; Delignières et al., 1998; Irwin & Kerwin, 2005; Teulier et al., 1998; van Emmerik et al., 2004; Williams et al., 2012).

Studies have reported that novices often coordinate simple relations between the timing of events and between joint actions. For example, during the swing under parallel bars in the bent inverted hang position, Delignières et al. (1998) reported that experts produce a 2:1 frequency ratio of forcing actions between the vertical and pendular oscillations of the body's centre of mass. However, novices produced a 1:1 frequency ratio throughout early learning, meaning that their interaction with the task was less complex. A reduction in complexity is also seen in the relation between moving joints. Moving limbs at the same time and in the same direction is a simpler pattern to control than moving joints at other relative frequencies (Haken et al., 1985).

Bernstein (1967) suggested that learners 'freeze' movements of proximal joints and segments in order to create a simpler control solution. As learning progressed more proximal joints or segments are then 'freed'. While evidence of 'freezing' before 'freeing' has been provided for learning tasks such as throwing (McDonald et al., 1989); hand writing (Newell & van Emmerik, 1989); ski simulation (Verijken et al., 1992) and soccer kicking (Davids et al., 2000; Chow et al., 2006), it is not unequivocal. For example, greater ranges of motion at proximal joints have been identified during the learning of giant swings (Williams et al., 2012). Therefore, evidence suggests that these phenomena are task specific. For example, 'freeing' might include swinging skills, where the body is acted on by gravity as a series of linked segments, while 'freezing' might occur in more advanced skills such as dismounting from high bar.

Specific constraints are the source of these movement pattern characteristics during learning, whether they be neural, creating a 'control' problem for the learner, or biomechanical, such as the ability to produce large joint kinetics (Williams et al., 2009; Williams et al., 2012). Simple frequencies and patterns of 'freezing' and 'freeing' of limb movements during learning are characteristics that can be subjectively assessed by a coach watching performers or objectively assessed by a biomechanist. It should also be noted that constraints of individual performers lead to different learning pathways in terms of both performance and technique changes, i.e. we are all individuals (Williams et al., 2012).

Variability in technique and performance outcome are key issues for contemporary motor learning researchers and provide useful information for the coaching process (van Emmerik & van Wegen, 2000; Newell et al., 2009; Bartlett et al., 2007; Newell et al., 2012; Hiley et al., 2013). The non-linear nature of changes in technique and performance outcome has been highlighted (Button et al., 2006; Robins et al., 2006; Bradshaw et al., 2007; Wilson et al., 2008; Newell et al., 2012). For example, high technique variability is evident when exploring the environment during early learning, while the performance outcome is also highly variable at this stage (Chow et al., 2008; Wilson et al., 2008; Williams et al., 2010).

Intermediate performance has been characterised by a more stable technique, with less variability, while the stability of the task outcome also increases (Wilson et al., 2008). Interestingly, highly skilled performers have been reported to increase technique variability in order to perform a consistently stable performance outcome during changing constraints (Arutyunyan et al., 1969; Bernstein, 1967; Wilson et al., 2008; Broderick & Newell, 1999; Chow et al., 2006). Consideration of technique variability and the non-linear changes in performance outcome during skill learning should be taken into account in training and physical preparation. Flexibility and exploration of techniques during early learning are advocated. In addition, the non-linear nature of change in performance outcome should be taken into account during gymnastic assessment, where the consistency of performance outcome might be more telling than that of a single trial (Newell et al., 2012).

It is the role of the coach to overcome the novice characteristics and guide a learner to a more technically correct technique. In gymnastics changes in technique are encouraged through learning progressions. Progressions are tasks or drills used to elicit changes in technique and performance in a safe efficient and effective manner. The progressions available to the coach are often based on his or her own knowledge and conceptual understanding of the key movement patterns and body positions; and the timings of the key actions of the final skill (Irwin et al., 2005). The conceptual understanding is influence by 4 themes; current coaching knowledge; progressions and training already known; a mental picture; and a descriptive biomechanical understanding of the final skill.

Irwin and Kerwin (2005) ranked methodical progressions based on their (biomechanical) similarity to the final skill. Because gymnasts are training near bio-physical limits, the need to identify an effective pathway of skill development is desirable. Replication of the spatio and temporal characteristics of the target skill in the progressions was identified as fundamental to this process. In addition, similarity in joint coordination and bioenergetics between the progressions and the target skill alongside the biological variability was examined (Irwin & Kerwin, 2007a, b). This objective method of choosing and developing skill progressions is useful for coaches and biomechanists whose primary aim is to make training as safe and effective as possible.

A challenge for coaches and applied biomechanists is to understand and communicate theoretically grounded information from motor learning and biomechanics in a meaningful and effective way in order that it can inform more efficient and effective training.

9.5 Conclusion

This chapter has examined some of the major contemporary issues in gymnastics research (coaching biomechanics interface, complex skills analysis, and skill development and learning). The chapter started with an overview of the coaching biomechanics interface and highlighted how this can be used to build a conceptual link between biomechanics and coaching knowledge. The area of complex skill analysis was discussed which provided insights into the link between similar skills and how more complex skills emerge naturally as gymnasts and coaches seek to optimise performance. Finally the issues surrounding skill development and learning are introduced to explain how this interesting and relevant theoretical area can inform coaches decisions. The application of these scientific principles form the future of gymnastics coaching.

References

Arutyunyan, G. H., Gurfinkel, V. S., & Mirskii, M. L. (1968). Investigation of aiming at a target. *Biophysics, 13*, 536-538.

Bartlett, R., Wheat, J., & Robins, M. (2007). Is movement variability important for sports biomechanists? *Sports Biomechanics, 6*(2), 224-243.

Bernstein, N. (1967). *The co-ordination and regulation of movements*. Oxford: Pergamon.

Bradshaw, E. J., Maulder, P. S., & Keogh, J. W. L. (2007). Biological movement variability during the sprint start: performance enhancement or hindrance? *Sports Biomechanics, 6*(3), 246-260.

Broderick, M. P., & Newell, K. M. (1999). Coordination patterns in ball bouncing as a function of skill. *Journal of Motor Behavior, 31*(2), 165-188.

Button, C., McLeod, M., Sanders, R., & Coleman, S. (2003). Examining movement variability in the basketball free-throw action at different skill levels. *Research Quarterly for Exercise and Sport, 74*(3), 257-269.

Caillou, N., Nouritt, D., Deschamps, T., Lauriot, B., & Delignieres, D. (2002). Overcoming spontaneous patterns of coordination during the acquisition of a complex balancing task. *Canadian Journal of Experimental Psychology, 56*, 284-294.

Chen, H. H., Liu, Y. T., Mayer-Kress, G., & Newell, K. M. (2005). Learning the pedalo locomotion task. *Journal of Motor Behavior, 37*, 247-256.

Chow, J. Y., Davids, K., Button, C., & Koh, M. (2006). Organization of motor system degrees of freedom during the Soccer Chip: an analysis of skilled performance. *International Journal of Sport Psychology, 37*, 207–229.

Delignières, D., Nourrit, D., Sioud, R., Leroyer, P., Zattara, M., & Micaleff, J. P. (1998). Preferred coordination modes in the first steps of learning a complex gymnastics skill. *Human Movement Science, 17*(2), 221-224.

Haken, H., Kelso, J. A. S., & Bunz, H. (1985). A theoretical model of phase-transitions in human hand movements. *Biological Cybernetics, 51*, 347-356.

Hiley, M. J., Zuevsky, V. V., & Yeadon, M. R. (2013). Is skilled technique characterized by high or low variability? An analysis of high bar giant circles. *Human Movement Science, 32*, 171-180.

Irwin, G., & Kerwin, D. G. (2007a). Inter-segmental coordination in progressions for the longswing on high bar. *Sports Biomechanics, 6*, 131-144.

Irwin, G., & Kerwin, D. G. (2007b). Musculoskeletal demands of progressions for the longswing on high bar. *Sports Biomechanics, 6*, 361-374.

Irwin, G., & Kerwin, D. G. (2005). Biomechanical similarities of progressions for the longswing on high bar. *Sports Biomechanics, 4*, 163-144.

Irwin, G., Hanton, S., & Kerwin, D. G. (2005). The conceptual process of skill progression development in artistic gymnastics. *Journal of Sports Sciences, 23*, 1089-1099.

Ko, Y-G., Challis, J. H., & Newell, K. M. (2003). Learning to coordinate redundant degrees of freedom in a dynamic balance task. *Human Movement Science, 22*, 47-66.

McDonald, P. V., van Emmerik, R. E. A., & Newell, K. M. (1989). The effects of practice on limb kinematics in a throwing task. *Journal of Motor Behavior, 21*, 245-264.

Newell, K. M. (1985). Coordination, control and skill. In D. Goodman., I. Franks, & R. B. Wilberg (Eds.), *Differing perspectives in motor learning, memory and control* (pp. 295-318). Amsterdam: North Holland.

Newell, K. M. (1986). Constraints on the development of coordination. In M. G. Wade, & H. T. A. Whiting (Eds.), *Motor development in children. Aspects of coordination and control* (pp. 341-360). Dordrecht, Netherlands: Martinus Nijhoff.

Newell, K. M., & Liu, Y-T. (2012). Functions of learning and the acquisition of motor skills (with reference to sport). *The Open Sports Science Journal, 5*(1-M3), 17-25.

Newell, K. M., & van Emmerik, R. E. A. (1989). The acquisition of coordination: preliminary analysis of learning to write. *Human Movement Science, 8*, 17–32.

Newell, K. M., Mayer-Kress, G., Hong, S. L., & Liu, Y-H. (2009). Adaptation and learning: characteristic time scales of performance dynamics. *Human Movement Science, 28*, 655-587.

Robins, M., Wheat, J. S., Irwin, G., & Bartlett, R. M. (2006). The effect of shooting distance on movement variability in basketball. *Human Movement Studies, 20*, 218–238.

Teulier, C., & Delignières, D. (2007). The nature of transition between novice and skilled coordination during learning to swing. *Human Movement Science, 23*(3), 376-392.

van Emmerik, R. E. A., & van Wegen, E. E. H. (2000). On variability and stability in human movement. *Journal of Applied Biomechanics, 16*, 394-406.

van Emmerik, R. E. A., Rosenstein, M. T., McDermott, W. J., & Hamill, J. (2004). A non linear dynamics approach to human movement. *Journal of Applied Biomechanics, 20*, 396-420.

Vereijken, B., van Emmerik, R. E. A., Whiting, H. T. A., & Newell, K. M. (1992). Free(z)ing degrees of freedom in skill acquisition. *Journal of Motor Behavior, 24*, 133-142.

Williams, G., Irwin. G., & Kerwin, D. G. (2009). The influence of experience on functional phase kinematics of the longswing. In A.J Harrison, R. Anderson, & I. Kenny (Eds.), *Proceedings of the 28th International Society of Biomechanics in Sport Conference* (pp. 696). Limerick, Ireland. ISBS.

Williams, G., Irwin. G., Kerwin, D. G., & Newell, K. M. (2012). Kinematic changes during learning the longswing on high bar. *Sports Biomechanics, 11*(1), 20-33.

Wilson, C., Simpson, S. E., van Emmerik, R.E.A., & Hamill, J. (2009) Coordination variability and skill development in expert triple jumpers. *Sports Biomechanics, 7*(1), 2-9.

CHAPTER 10

REFLECTIONS ON PLANNING AND CONTROL OF SPORT TRAINING IN RHYTHMIC GYMNASTICS.

Mélix Ilisástigui Avilés, Yolaini Govea Díaz & Nelly Ochoa Borrás

University of Sciences of the Physical Culture and the Sport "Manuel Fajardo"
(Cuba).
Correspondence to: melix@uccfd.cu

10.1 Introduction

Rhythmic gymnastics is a sport where art and technique are blended, and the gymnasts outcomes depend on the development of those two components, which are expressed in the composition and execution of the competitive exercises. This conjugation depends on several factors, such as the occurrence of these two elements in the composition and execution of competitive exercises. When a gymnast arrives at the stage of 'mastery' (after eight to ten years of systematic training), she already possesses a maximum level of gymnastic technique. Therefore, she is oriented to the improvement of the competitive exercise, in each competitive event program. According to this objective, all the training cycles in rhythmic gymnastics are planned and controlled by the coach, adapting them to the individual strengths and weaknesses of each gymnast (and/or her corresponding team or group). This should be done with regard to the demands manifested in the Code of Points of the Olympic cycle. In this chapter, several characteristics are mentioned that include the planning and the control as a part of the process of training in rhythmic gymnastics. Experiences that emerge from a scientific investigation of a group of Cuban researchers are presented in greater detail.

10.2 Planning of sport training in rhythmic gymnastics

In the training process in rhythmic gymnastics, planning is considered by different authors as one of the essential elements therein. There are different approaches concerning this aspect but the authors of this chapter highlight the definition of García and Cols (1996) who state: "planning of sport training represents a plan or action project that is carried out with the process of a sportsman's training in order to obtain a certain objective (high performance)." The authors also refer to the definition given by Sánchez (1994) about planning of training: "it is the process by means of which the coach looks for and determines, with more probability, alternative and ways of action that can lead to the success". Furthermore, Laffranchi (2001) argues that: "planning means to collect, to control and to analyze the data obtained during the training of a season with the objective of accompanying the development of work and performance of the gymnast's technique."

The development and structuring of gymnastics preparation as any process can be understood as a system that is based on the information obtained previously (diagnosis), leading to several necessities that may affect performance on a short-, medium-, and long-term perspective, where its main components are: programming, realization, control, analysis, and correction (of the training process). Programming and diagnosis are integrated into the process of planning as separate components of the process. Besides the denomination of the process of guiding preparation, other authors identify the prospective dimension of the process, and inside it, the predictive role of planning, which should be based on the results of scientific investigations, considering the aspects such as the accumulation of information (e.g., the evolution of the sport, and the evolution of the recent methods for preparation in high performance gymnastics), the analysis of the best teams and gymnasts in the world, national, state or regional level (e.g., strengths and weaknesses), the analysis of changes in the structure of the own teams, and of each gymnast (classification, winning the championships, goals, and individual objectives).

Among the aspects that we have to keep in mind for planning, are those that traditionally have been used in training, such as the desired objective that should be reached, the ultimate state of the previous cycle, the convocation of the competition, the results of last controls, the level of the competition, and the available time to achieve the objective, and others. There are also other aspects, including internal or external contradictions sustaining the formulation of the objective (demanding level of competition and gymnast's real level), functions that gymnasts will carry out in the competition, selection criteria and organization of content in order to reach an objective, and the trends in the national or international system for participating in competition.

Structure and content are two important elements that are presented in the training planning: the first one refers to different forms of organizing the available time for preparation and competitions, and the second refers to the training orientations. Nowadays, the frequency of competitions always force the coaches and the gymnasts to be prepared for each event. Therefore, other forms of structuring and planning, according to the characteristics of each sport specificity have arisen.

A great number of variables affect the planning process making it hard to accomplish all the demands of the planning. Nevertheless, planning training in rhythmic gymnastics should be practiced and also understood as a flexible process that allows for necessary adjustments, since what has been planned is done. According to Garcia et al (1996), two aspects have to be considered: execution and evaluation. Execution aims at realising the maximum outlined in the initial plan. On the other hand, even though the outcomes predicted were reached, it will be incomplete unless a regular process evaluation is done in order to allow the correction of faults or ensure the efficacy of it. In contradiction to the mentioned aspects, Forteza (1999) considers that:

Planning and control of sport training in rhythmic gymnastics. 181

> "All the information taken to the plan of session is important, but a plan should be operative and dynamic, and the most important thing that is susceptible to be controlled, that is to say, the plan should specify very well the object - content - method, because this is the pedagogic relationship that will allow to reach the conclusions of the increase or possible decrease of sport performance in the controls that we make"". ... a plan is real the extent to which it is susceptible to be controlled" (p. 192).

This confirms the self-regulating role of control, but on the other hand it implies a high level of rigour and objectivity during the planning process. Deciding on how to plan, we should keep in mind the different models of training (according to the characteristics of sport in general and of gymnastics in particular). In rhythmic gymnastics the use of extensive loads in training has prevailed according to the theory of Matveev, and it continues to be valid for any preparation level, particularly at the basic motor development. However, among elite gymnasts, other methods have been used as the concentrated load training system, but suitable only for the high performance level. This fact, allows the increasing speed of the sport training process. Therefore, the key for success is the technique perfection and the proper use of the integrated systems of planning with a high level of specificity according to the gymnats' level, the competition level, and the time for preparation. There are several aspects that should be highlighted:

- The increase of training load to excessive, and non considerate levels in previous decades: Increasing training loads should not be made without any reference to individual characteristics such as biological and chronological age, yet in regard to the results of the different applied tests.

- Training should be planned in terms of the general, yet functional, direction, since this has a better validity as compared to an isolated planning of single components of the preparation. The baseline would be the elements of the energetic substrates and the metabolic trace left in the gymnast body after each physical exercise, as for organization as for preparation control.

- In this sense, the definitions of determined directions of performance (DDP) and conditioned directions of performance (CDP) in rhythmic gymnastics are important, as such as the characteristics of the competitive exercise. According to investigations carried out by Ameller (2005) and Ochoa (2011), for the rhythmic gymnastics the definitions are: DDP - flexibility (active-passive), coordinative ability and strength in general and explosive strength, anaerobic endurance, effective technique, teaching: body technique - technique of apparatuses, competition; CDP - resistance to strength, aerobic endurance, speed.

- Increase of the effectiveness of execution of competitive exercises is a premise to reach high scores.

According to Ameller (2005) planning at the beginning of a training cycle, is more centered in learning and stabilisation of new technical skills and in the development of the general and specific motor abilities for the activity, with a trend towards the use of special means. Planning isolated elements and repetitions is good to consolidate basic technique and it should take a high priority place in the first stage of the preparation, and since the beginning a logical requirement surrounding the gymnast individual potential and the learning stages should appear. Combinations of elements (1/2 and 1/3) is a characteristic of a special meso-cycle. The polish of skills is characterized by high volume of repetitions and by the quality control of skills as the determinant to accomplish the load. Repetition of competitive exercises in its entirety is manifested fundamentally in the meso-cycle (polish, stability, control, pre-competitive and competitive, and the execution is determined by the competitive objectives).

10.3 Example of a planning system for directions of sport training in rhythmic gymnastics (Ochoa, 2011)

When it is impossible to work with long cycles preparation due to the lack of time to achieve the objective of the competitive prepartion, a model planning ATR can be selected (accumulation, transformation, and realization) with the integration of planning for training directions, which constitutes itself as a work system never used before by the CubanTechnical Committee. The theoretical analysis, used as the antecedent of the model system, make possible the isolated quantification of the specific components particular to the methodological concepts of the structure and the contente on the sport trainning planning, while the focus on the system make possible the understanding of these components and their inter-relationships as a actual integration (see Figure 10.1).

Although the use of this type of planning in this sport is unusual, it was decided to use it in order to be more objective and because it determines the global work direction as well as the amount of work in each one phase.

To determine the percentages by directions and their transversal and longitudinal behaviour the diagnosis antecedents of the subjects was considered in order to potenctialize the amount of work (volume) indicated by the directions and the relation to the partial objec-

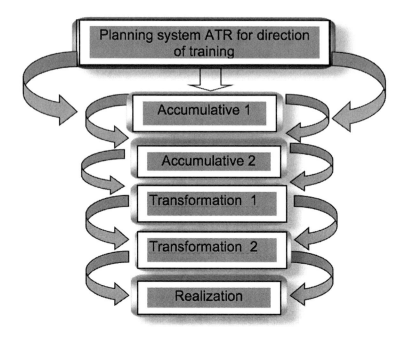

Figure 10.1: Graphic example of the structure used for planning of training in rhythmic gymnastics.

tive. Moreover, the fundamental criteria to manipulate the dependent variable of the percentage distribution was considered in each meso structure related to the same total time percentage. This was based on the methodological treatment of directions proposed by Fortaleza (1999), and on the planning of the pyramidal structure, in which the DDR in the meso structure are always larger than 50% in relation to CDP, whilst their overall limit represents 100% (Forteza, 1999). In light of this definition, in the first accumulative meso-cycle, decisive directions were planned to 70% of the total time, and conditions to 30%. In the second accumulative meso-cycle, decisive directions accounted for 80% of the total time whilst conditions accounted for

20%. The meso-cycles 'Transformation 1' and 'Transformation 2' the author argued, that for decisive directions 90% of the total time should be spent whilst for the conditions the remaining 10% should be spent. In the final meso-cycle (realization) the decisive part cumulates to 95%, and conditions comprise 5% of the total time.

10.4 Control and their characteristics in rhythmic gymnastics

Sport training as a pedagogic process requires control and in this respect Harre (1983) outlines that it is important to control the performance of each one of the athletes by means of measures, the counting, the observation, and evaluation in sport or in any discipline with the objective of verifying the effect of each loads or the state of each athlete's training. This argumentation is confirmed by Godik (1989) who considers control and planning of loads as important components inside sport training. He also said that selection and evaluation of indicators for control are in the dependence of the characteristics of each sport.

In this respect also Mena (n.d.) outlines that control is a more general category derived from the the role of orientation of sport preparation, with the complemented by evaluation procedures and measurements. The same author outlines that the role of direction control is observed in the athletes errors correction, in the precision of the execution, in any proposal for the planning change, and it may be accompanied by an evaluation criteria when required.

Analysing the criteria previously presented by different authors, we observe that there are convergent points when considering control as a process that offers information on the assimilation of the applied loads for each athlete. This allows coaches to make the necessary decisions to setup training in a functional, yet bio-positive, referring to knowledge of how a gymnasts' body has adapted to applied training loads.

The indicators of states and effects of training registered during control are compared with the results reached in competitive exercises and with quantitative and qualitative characteristics of load. In general, based on the results of this comparison, they drive decisions that, in their completed form, are presented as training plans and training programs.

In this respect, Mesa (2007) refers that convergence exists among authors like García, Grosser, Harre, Platonov and Mata stating that the main objective of the periodization of the controls is to determine the objectives of the preparation. Therefore, controlling can be implemented in the moment of preparation, or when it will be necessary to check the execution of the proposed objectives, as these are the ones which rule the process of athlete preparation and will be proved during the control. This is most helpful for the coach in terms of feedback procedures and in the regulation of the training process. Controlling competitive exercises during the preparation, is considered as a necessary activity whilst keeping in mind the diverse indicators of physical, physiological, and psychological load at the same time.

Godik (1989) outlines that: "for the control of competitive exercise it is necessary to know the structure and factors that condition their result. This information allows to direct the training process in a given moment, as well as to predict the requirements that will rule the competitive exercise loads for the athletes' body, from higher results up to the world records.

Controlling to accomplish the objective is currently the most used way in the artistic and competitive sport and for so, many working hours are necessary, at least six hours per day. It does, however, play an important role in the creation of individual planning. Without individual plans, it is nearly impossible to follow the purposes of a general plan. The constant strive for perfection in the execution of technical elements constitutes an objective and fundamental direction in the preparation of rhythmic gymnast.

Evaluation still constitutes a permanent aspect of controlling the training load from the beginning of preparation for which parameters of technical efficiency are settle down. The recognition of the execution quality, the efficacy of the technical actions conditioned to the exact accomplishment of the movement directions, within the range and time, is something that constitutes the permanent evaluation of the accomplishment of the partial and final objectives.

Efficiency is an indicator of the execution of the load that regulates the intensity in achievement of the objective. It means that each repetition should fulfil certain qualitative aspects so that it is considered as a functional load. This is conditioned to each work stage and it is dependent on the methodological criteria to win or improve the technical difficulties and composition requirements. Technical efficiency is understood as the possibility to carry out certain actions without errors and with high level of interpretation, conditioned to the gymnast's physical-technical and psychological possibilities.

According to the criteria expressed by Ameller (2005) sustained in her experience as a rhythmic gymnastics coach in the preparation of the Cuban team, the achievement of technical efficiency is related to execution, which is controlled through effective technical DDP. It is developed in the following stages:

- Learning stage: Control of certain objectives of technique (70%-85%).

- Improvement stage: Eliminating unnecessary actions (90%-95%).

- Stabilization stage: Impeccable performance with high artistic expression (+95%)

In order to increase the continuous effectiveness of elements and combinations during preparation, several control procedures exist, such as testing the effectiveness for elements and combinations, controlling the execution of halves or thirds, or controlling the relationships among two or more elements.

According to Godik (1989), the intensity of the physiological load during exercise is determined by the magnitude of the morphofunctional systems which rule the body. In this sense, quantities of competitive exercise may serve as a basis for the calculation of the relative intensity and thus for the load. The author argues that intensity of effort in gymnastics is based on the number of elements as well as combinations in a given amount of time.

This approach is not considered valid for every period or stage of gymnastic preparation, because the number of elements and combinations that comprise the competitive exercise are always executed with the same duration. We can see some variation in training competitive exercises in its qualitative aspect, and there is no reference of values that can take the internal or physiological indicators when applying this training load.

In rhythmic gymnastics usually the quantity of elements or sequences are analysed, revealing that larger values are often found in the final part of the general preparation (quantity of single elements)

Planning and control of sport training in rhythmic gymnastics. 189

and at the end of the stage of special preparation (quantity of routines). When the magnitude of external load is quantified in training the different elements are counted and aspects such as the quantity of repetitions are calculated (balances, turns, jumps, launchings, dance skills, etc.). In the case of longer sequences or complete routines each part or each half part can be counted and the quantity of repetitions can be calculated.

Regarding the intensity as a qualitative indicator of training load, Bompa, mentioned by Forteza, outlines that "intensity refers to the quality of work carried out in a period of time". Furthermore, Ranzola and Barrios (1998) consider that "intensity is the specificity of influence of magnitude of the content load and its duration". García et al. (1996) coincides with other authors when he considers intensity as a qualitative aspect of load that is subordinated to the athlete's level and at the moment of the season.

In rhythmic gymnastics, Laffranchi (2001) highlights procedures that can be used for progression of training load or increment of intensity in this sport. These procedures are the following: (1) execution of isolated elements without making mistakes, (2) increasing the number of repetitions of whole exercises, (3) execution of whole exercises without making an error, (4) increasing the speed of execution of elements from the general and specific physical preparation, (5) execution of body elements used in composition without errors, and (6) reducing the intervals of rest among whole exercises.

With the objective of achieving a better quality in the execution we began to use methods of 'continuous effectiveness', and 'effectiveness 10' since the 1990's. The first mentioned method consists of carrying out a certain amount of elements, combinations, half or whole routines in a correct and consecutive way. 'Effectiveness 10' comprises carrying out 10 elements or combinations with absolute effectiveness whilst being able to vary them in a situation-dependent manner. Although these methods contributed to the improvement of quality in the execution of exercises, they are highly effective only when applied during the initial stage of special preparation.

10.5 Methodological example for controlling intensity of training of individual competitive exercises in rhythmic gymnastics (see Govea, 2011)

Cuban technical staff considered that the forms of controlling the competitive exercises intensity during special preparation were not enough for the purposes stated recently. Then, based on the determined indicators that are considered to control individual intensity, it was designed a method which included the procedure and needed elements to control the load by evaluating systematically and quantifying the concerned corrections in the planning.

Based on the results obtained in the diagnosis and considering both the characteristics of the competitive exercise and the lack of the methodological procedures carried out by the rhythmic gymnastics coaches, indicators that should complement the actual model were determined. These indicators should also satisfy the trends of the contemporary competitive requirements, as the non existance of the single declared and recognised model was proved for this sport.

Control the intensity of competitive exercises is associated to theoretical approaches dealing with feedback and as pedagogical control. The coach will usually make the necessary decisions to setup the training process based on a systematic analysis that incorporates aspects such as biological adaptation as well as the control and technical effectiveness of the execution.

The methodology that is exposed here, is not considered single and complete. It has, however, a flexible and integral character because during special preparation it can be adapted according to each gymnast's level, to the demands of a particular competitive event, and even to the coach's objectives. The ultimate objective can be formulated as follows: Controlling the intensity of training of competitive exercises of the Cuban elite gymnasts by determining the values that represent specific indicators and the relationships among them (Govea, 2001, p. 92).

The methodology will be implemented from the moment the gymnast carries out her complete routine with music as a competition exercise. The routine should not be subjected to further changes. Repetitions of the competitive exercise are to be performed with the aim of perfect technical execution. The coach is then advised to execute the following steps for the sake of controlling the training intensity of these exercises:

Step 1: The coach is advised to determine the content of the competitive exercises. This may comprise analysing factors such as the total amount of elements, the quantity and value of elements that mainly contribute to the difficulty of the routine, the duration of competitive exercise, and more. In order to determine the total number of elements it is advised to quantify separately the elements that still can become linking elements or difficult. Elements can furthermore be evaluated according to the execution requirements.

Step 2: The coach is advised to define the execution, quality, and their corresponding influences of exercise during trainings. Heart frequency can for instance be the physiological indicator that will allow to evaluate the response of the gymnasts' body in each repetition of competitive exercises. The heart rate at the beginning (f1) and at the end (f2) of the competitive exercise is noted and the difference will be calculated to obtain the increment of heart rate. The analysis of f1 behaviour in connection with the best qualification during trainings allows to know with what rate the gymnast execution of exercise should begin to obtain a better qualification. The increment of heart rate should also be analysed in connection with best scores reached by the gymnast in each session of training. Heart rate during f2 will allow to estimate the effect in gymnast's body in relation to the load. These values are usually expected to be in an area of high intensity (180-200 bpm), which can be supported from investigating the best Cuban individual gymnasts in the last 2 Olympic cycles. Values outside the mentioned range are admitted because they could, among other, depend on individual gymnasts' characteristics or on other variables such as psychological disposition, level of gymnast's preparation, training session schedule, and errors that alter logical sequence of exercises, which should be controlled in order to accomplish the purposes of the stage.

Step 3: The coach is advised to evaluate the intensity of competitive exercises. Intensity is defined as follows: Intensity = % effectiveness of final note (Nf) / physiologic answer (Inc.Fc). The value of 'Intensity' is characterised as follows:

- 'Good': When the planned objective is completed between 90 and 100%.

- 'Regular': When the planned objective is completed between 80 and 90%.

- 'Bad': When the planned objective is completed less than 79%.

Methods: Statistics (descriptive statistic). To evaluate the intensity, all f2 values as well as the final scores of each repetition should be averaged. Additionally, the relative amount to which the objective was completed should be calculated, for events in each training session, and when concluding each micro cycle.

Step 4: The coach is advised to provide feedback derived from the obtained results, as well as carry out changes in planning and/or in defining the objectives for individual gymnasts and/or a group of gymnasts.

10.6 Final considerations

We argue that it is necessary to integrate the methodological approaches and/or the data from scientific investigations in the training process in rhythmic gymnastics, in order to follow the contemporary scenario of the gymnasts competitive preparation. This is especially true when it comes to the development and evolution of new scenarios. Current trends and tendencies of planning in rhythmic gymnastics are predominantly based on theories of Matveev. However, one needs to acknowledge the structural advantages as well as the advantages with regards to the content of the ATR model of Issurin and Kaverin (1986) in connection with the development of the preparation in short periods of time and the possibility of increasing the specific content which are characteristics of the sport and starting from the integration of the planning according to the direction of performance.

The methodology for control of intensity constitutes an useful tool for control of intensity of the competitive exercises training in elite rhythmic gymnasts, allowing for a systematic control during training competitive exercises.

References

Ameller, K. S. (2005). *Planning and their characteristics in rhythmic gymnastics.* Conference for sport trainers. UCCFD "Manuel Fajardo", Havana, Cuba.

Forteza de la Rosa, A. (2001). *Sport Training. Science and technological innovation.* Havana: Editorial Cientifico Tecnica.

Forteza de la Rosa, A (2009). *Sport Training. High methodology and planning.* Colombia: Editorial Kinesis.

García Manso, J.M., Navarro, M., & Ruíz , J.A. (1996). *Planing of the sport training.* Madrid Spain: Sport Editorial Gymnos, S.L

Govea Y. (2011). *Methodology for the control of the intensity of training of individual competitive exercises in elites Cuban gymnasts of Rhythmic Gymnastics.* (Doctoral dissertation). Havana. UCCFD "Manuel Fajardo", Cuba.

Grosser, M., Starischka, S., & Zimmermann, E. (1992). *Principles of sport training.* Barcelona, Spain: Editions Rock, INC.

Harre, D. (1983). *Theory of sport training.* Havana: Editorial cientifico tecnica.

Ilisástigui M., & Govea Y. (2011). Planning and control of sport training in rhythmic gymnastics. *EFDeportes.com, Digital Magazine. Buenos Aires, Year 16, N° 162.* Available at: http://www.efdeportes.com.

Laffranchi, B. (2001). *Sport Training applied to rhythmic gymnastics.* Londrina: UNOPAR.

Mena Hernández, M. (1999). *Control and evaluation, direction elements and regulation of training process.* Conference for sport trainers. ISCF "Manuel Fajardo" UPCSS, Havana, Cuba.

Platonov, V. N. (1988). *Sport training. Theory and Methodology* (3rd ed.). Barcelona: Editorial Paidotribo.

Ochoa, N. (2011). *System of planning for direction of sport training in the Rhythmic Gymnastics (Specialty of Group).* (Master's thesis). Havana. UCCFD "Manuel Fajardo" UPCSS, Cuba.

Ukran. M. L. (n.a.). *Methodology of training of the gymnasts.* Editorial Pueblo y Educacion.

CHAPTER 11

PSYCHOLOGICAL ASPECTS IN THE SPORT PREPARATION OF BRAZILIAN WOMEN GYMNASTS PARTICIPATING IN THE OLYMPIC GAMES: THE GYMNASTS' VIEW

Laurita Marconi Schiavon

State University of São Paulo - Biosciences Institute (Brazil).
Correspondence to: lauritaschi@hotmail.com

11.1 Introduction

Psychological factors are widely taken into account in sport nowadays, just due to the fact they often differentiate between athletes at the same physical and technical levels. Besides, tolerance to the training hours over the years and the pressure from coaches, parents, the media, friends, and oneself for results lead boredom and stress to be components often observed in training. Brandão (2005, p. 111) comments on this issue: "Sport training means a daily job, for several hours and a long period. It's a process which submits the body to high physical and psychological loads in order to increase the athlete's work capacity".

The fact that artistic gymnastics (AG) is a modality consisting of complex skills and accuracy, which involve the gymnast's safety, also causes anxiety with regard to the exercises to be performed: fear or lack of confidence. There're studies on this issue and, according to Brandão (2005), the most common fears in AG are: failing, obtaining unsuccessful results, making simple mistakes, executing risky movements, being rejected by the coach, getting injured, competition, the unknown, getting nervous during competition, getting unable to sleep at the night before competition, talking to the coach, being unable to fulfill what is expected from her/him, obtaining scores which don't contribute to the team, falling down, and competing in a bad way, wrongly performing a movement, being rejected by the environment (relatives, peers, etc.), getting sick, the referees, the future (Brandão, 2005).

This chapter addresses important psychological aspects surrounding women's artistic gymnastics (WAG) athletes, as well as the psychological preparation during the sport career of the ten brazilian female athletes participating in the Olympic Games from 1980 to 2004, in order to register and analyze them under the light of sport pedagogy. It's derived from a broader research carried out as a doctoral thesis, entitled "Artistic Gymnastics and Oral History: sport training of brazilian female athletes participating in the Olympic Games (1980-2004)" (Schiavon, 2009).

This research was conducted through the Oral History method (Meihy, 2005; Simson, 1988; Thompson, 2002). One resorted to the use of this method mainly because there's no available record on the sport training of these female gymnasts, whether documents or other published researches; besides, it's possible, through the indicated method, to survey detailed information with regard to the events experienced in the sport career of each of the female gymnasts, who, otherwise, wouldn't be noticed.

Among the various techniques for applying and utilizing the Oral History method, the "oral testimony" was adopted in this research, where the researcher proposes a theme to organize the life report of people under study (Queiroz, 1988, p. 21). The research, in a broader way, focused on the "sport life story" of these female gymnasts and, more specifically in this chapter, the theme addressed, generated through the testimonies, was "psychological aspects in the gymnasts' sport training".

Ten female gymnasts participated in the research; they're presented in chronological order of participation in the Olympic Games: Cláudia Magalhães (1980), Tatiana Figueiredo (1984), Luisa Parente (1988 and 1992), Soraya Carvalho (1996), Daniele Hypólito (2000, 2004, 2008, and 2012), Camila Comin (2000 and 2004), Ana Paula Rodrigues (2004), Caroline Molinari (2004), Daiane dos Santos (2004, 2008, and 2012), and Laís Souza (2004 and 2008).[1] The criterion set for determining the research universe was: female brazilian gymnasts participating in (or classified to) the Olympic Games, in the women's artistic gymnastics modality by the year 2004.

Among the ways how Oral History may be constructed, cross-analysis was the technique adopted in this research, where "oral evidence is regarded as an information source from which an expositive text is organized" (Thompson, 2002, p. 304). In general, one compares the evidence from an interview to those from another one, and associates it to the evidence from other sources, whenever possible, disagreeing, confirming, or even collaborating with new approaches, which may point out the pathway towards a new interpretation (Thompson, 2002).

For comparison between the collaborators in this study, they were grouped by similarities in their histories as a whole, an inherent characteristic of Oral History as a way for evaluating the coherence of testimonies (Thompson, 2002). Thus, there emerged three distinct groups, which received the following nomenclatures: "pioneering gymnasts" (three), "transition gymnasts" (four), and "new generation gymnasts" (three).

11.2 Theoretical framework

Arkaev and Suchilin (2004) expose the work developed with the Russian AG team and report that they don't provide a psychological preparation disconnected from other ones. They warn that gymnasts need

---

[1] The gymnasts have authorized the use of their names for scientific purposes, important information for Oral History studies, which usually present the names of exposed individuals, due to their importance. Since there aren't numerous subjects in this kind of qualitative research, it's important to highlight their relevance to the research context, in this case, the women's artistic gymnastics in Brazil.

to learn dealing with psychological preparation along with technical, tactical, physical preparation, etc. The authors aren't followers of the sport psychologists' participation when working with the specific features of the modality conducted during the very training sessions. The competition AG situations are quite predictable (stable environment) and the authors work with these situations to simulate competitions and stressful situations during the actual athlete's preparation. They take into account the fact that the coaches who trained the gymnasts since they were children, and took them to the top of sport, know the psychological nuances of each of them better than any other professional and they already know how to deal with each one.

At some moments of the process, the Russian team's coaches take into account the importance of a psychologist to determine and identify the psychological profiles within the Russian team. In these cases, individual psychological tests are conducted in order to evaluate the gymnast's personality, level of motivation to practice, speed to process visual information, evaluation of motor memory, and accuracy in movements which have already been mastered. They also think the psychologist is important to identify the psychological profiles of the great world champions, so they are also used as parameters (Arkaev & Suchilin, 2004).

According to Smoleuskiy and Gaverdouskiy (1996) there're studies pointing out psychological particularities in AG. According to the authors, the most striking features of the modality are: being "introverted", and the body itself is the object of consciousness and sensory perception; assimilation and execution of exercises take place according to psychological sensations; highly developed concentration and attention abilities during movements; well-developed predictive reactions (ability to evaluate the situation and decide the next movements to be performed[2]); accuracy and emotional stability; high mastery and volitional abilities (characteristic of high tension in the modality); being focused up to the point of "getting disconnected" from undesirable outside situations; and will for training and know how to distribute the gymnast's psychic energy, which is widely used in the modality, especially in the exercises involving greater risk, causing a frequent stress.

According to Mássimo (1996) many gymnasts feel they aren't ready for certain exercises, feel uncomfortable with regard to their fears, and are afraid to talk to their coaches about it. Gymnasts who don't feel able to talk about their fears are major candidates for injuries and safety risks. The fact that many gymnasts are afraid of "talking to their coaches" is a cultural feature in AG, obviously stimulated by the behavior and attitude of coaches with regard to young athletes. Open communication between coach and gymnast is directly related to psychological aspects and confidence. The gymnasts having more difficulty to talk to their coaches about their abilities need to be encouraged to do so.

Moreover, the same author stresses that gymnasts who train in a negative atmosphere and those who are constantly the subject of observations which make them "down" are more distracted and experience more emotional stress. Smoleuskiy and Gaverdouskiy (1996) also address this issue, emphasizing the need for education attitudes one the part of the coach, creating positive motivations for training and a favorable psychological environment for the group, without

---

[2] It isn't unusual that the gymnast is able to choose her moves at the competition time, but they can be changed if there's a need, such as an error in a sequence with important movements. The gymnast may include another move with the same characteristic if there's need and this had often been already predicted and trained during rehearsals.

disregarding the personality of each gymnast. Benk (2006) also highlights that a work towards a proper education can, undoubtedly, contribute so that the athlete appreciates her own effort, perseverance, and the development of her own skills, ensuring that she achieves the best possible performance.

Gervis and Dunn (2004) conducted a study in the United Kingdom on the emotional abuse of elite child athletes by their coaches and confirmed the lack of knowledge and/or adequate attitudes on the part of coaches when dealing with children in sport. The results of this study aimed to clarify the behavior of some coaches as a threat to the psychological well-being of young elite athletes. The authors studied former athletes from various modalities who were elite athletes between 8 and 16 years of age and had a 6 to 10-year career, and AG was among these modalities. One took into account in this study eight kinds of abusive behaviors: disdain, humiliate, scream, serve as "scapegoat", disregard, isolate, threaten, and ignore. All study athletes talked about some way to make them "down" or screams on the part of their coaches, 75% of subjects reported threatening and humiliation behaviors and half served as "scapegoats", feeling rejected and being ignored when they were elite young athletes. All subjects also reported that the coaches' behavior got worse when the athletes were identified as elite ones. As a result of this behavior on the part of coaches, the subjects felt stupid, worthless, less confident, lost, depressed, humiliated, fearful, and angry.

According to Gervis and Dunn (2004), there's a wide dissemination of results in sport, but this is different with regard to the methods to achieve success. "Training is always boring, repetitive, and lengthy. This is a physical and psychological demand which requires the athletes to try reaching extreme limits. Sport dominates their life and they're often socially isolated" (Gervis & Dunn, 2004, p. 216).

The relationship between coach and athlete may be the most significant relation the child has to an adult person. In fact, the athlete may see the coach as being more important than their own parents. Children who train six times a week spend more time with coaches than with their parents, something which generates a considerable influence on children and makes them vulnerable to abuses. And, often, the coaches' career itself depends on the result obtained by some athletes (Gervis & Dunn, 2004). The same authors explain that the most frequent kind of abuse by the coaches is screaming, as a subject reports: "He was always very aggressive, it frightened me a lot, I was afraid of doing everything because all I did was wrong, or all I did led him to scream with me" (Gervis & Dunn, 2004, p. 220).

Making someone down and humiliating her/him is a kind of abuse which can be felt long after the end of sport life, as reported by an athlete: "I think being humiliated is so horrible and I'll always remember the pain it causes" (Gervis & Dunn, 2004, p. 221).

Cathy McCoy, the gymnast cited earlier by Williams and Warkov (1995, p.134), exposes her experience:

> "The lesson I've learned more in sport - besides pleasure and motivation - is that if you work hard, you'll become better and better. And this finding, greatly stimulating confidence, especially for girls, is the positive side of the gymnastics. But I know there's also the negative side. I've seen girls lose confidence because of pressure and expectation. This happens when they practice sport for someone else in addition to themselves. They're afraid of letting their coach and their parents down, thus, they feel guilty and unsuccessful if they do it. And, almost always, as girls experience these pressure situations when they're very young, they don't know how to deal with them."

Gervis and Dunn (2004) stress that no one seems to question the coaches' behavior, this is accepted as being part of sport and it often takes place with "closed doors". Further studies are needed to emphasize and reveal this kind of situation, warning and clarifying the athletes' parents with regard to these events, as well as the coaches themselves about the damage this kind of behavior with athletes, especially in childhood.

11.3 Psychological aspects of female Brazilian athletes participating in the Olympic Games: cross-analysis

Several significant aspects related to the psychological preparation were approached by the collaborators in this study, divided into the three groups mentioned, depicting different moments of AG in Brazil through their account.[3]

In the brazilian pioneering AG generation, there wasn't sufficient or continued support to proper monitoring by sport psychology professionals. When this opportunity was made available in the gymnasts training, one can notice that there were occasional work and, perhaps, a lack of time to offer continuity and a psychological follow-up suitable for high sport performance gymnasts. The gymnasts' testimonies report some conditions:

> "In Universidade Gama Filho there was a sport medicine sector. I think there wasn't a psychologist. We helped each other and the master."
>
> "I did a lot of tests when they gathered the athletes in this CEFAM (Project Impact). They did everything: physical test, psychological

---
[3] It's worth stressing that all discussions start from the testimonials providing evidence through the gymnasts' view, who experienced this process; 3 out of the 10 gymnasts who were still active at the collection time and 7 out of them had already finished their careers. All of them were over 18 years of age.

test. They did a set of tests with us. [...] We had no psychological or nutritional follow-up, indeed."

"Several times, we had other kinds of support, such as the psychological one. [...] And many things, sometimes, was provided by the coach himself. [...] Anyway, it was a time when there was no structure. It's available now."

Among the transition gymnasts, one identifies that there was psychological support in the gymnasts' training only from the moment when they had the contribution of the AG Excellence Center, as one can notice in their testimonies:

"I've never had a psychological support. None."

"We had psychological support for four years, it was the period between the Olympic Games in Sydney and Athens, which was also crucial for us to maintain ourselves, knowing ourselves, know the difficulties, know how to wait, these were the main factors."

"We already had a psychological preparation with Ruth, who is still active. It was already available. In 2000, in fact, we started it."

Among the gymnasts from the new generation, psychological support was also provided by the Excellence Center only during the preparation for the Olympic Games in Athens:

"Regarding other professionals who work in the preparation for the Olympic Games, we had a psychologist in the year the Olympic Games were held. Every Wednesday we had a little meeting. She spoke to us, performed some tests, told some jokes. By the way, there's a painting there that we made with her, too. She talked and I think it helped a lot. It allowed us to go much calmer. It helped us a lot to reflect. It helped a lot. [...] The psychological work was conducted in group. And it was about gymnastics. Regarding personal life, she spoke individually. She took every one who had a problem and asked if there was anything wrong, she talked about personal life this way. In group, we talked about gymnastics, competitions, she asked how our week was going."

Often, the coaches themselves also end up conducting this psychological work with the gymnasts, due to lack of structure or financial resource for hiring a professional or by choice, as it used to happen in the former USSR and as it's happening now in Russia, according to information from Smoleuskiy and Gaverdouskiy (1996) and Arkaev and Suchilin (2004); the coaches choose not to have psychologists guiding gymnasts, because they think the coaches know the athletes better than anyone else, they are working together since the athletes' childhood. The coaches resort to sport psychologists only to perform psychological tests which determine the champions' profile, as well as those which detect and select sport talents.

The problem with this kind of option is that, despite really knowing the gymnasts, their attitude isn't always appropriate with regard to the event; often, they don't know how to handle situations which emerge in daily training sessions and in competitions. One of the "pioneering" gymnasts, commenting that she failed to keep a weight proper for the Olympic Games, as she fattened 2 kg in the Olympic Village, said:

> "And that wasn't all, indeed. There already was a strain, too. I was older, the coach wasn't able to control me anymore. There were other things which, somehow, may have negatively influenced. It wasn't related to concentration, because later on, during competition, you see good results, but it happened, this anxiety issue. Anxiety! I think this wasn't an isolated incident, there was something which generated anxiety and led me to be unable to control feeding."

The AG coach works for years with children, these children grow up and the treatment remains quite childish, a "maternal" relationship, as if it involved mother and daughter, with an authority constructed for years, which generates an insurmountable barrier. Gervis and Dunn (2004), studying the relationship between coach and athlete, explain that this it may be the most significant relationship the child has to an adult. In fact, the athlete can regard the coach as being more important than their own parents, [...] generating considerable influence on children and making them vulnerable to emotional abuse.

As mentioned in the literature review, Mássimo (1996) points out that the gymnasts who don't feel able to talk about their fears with their coaches are major candidates for injuries and safety risks. The fact that many gymnasts are afraid to talk to their coaches is a cultural aspect of AG, obviously stimulated by the behavior and attitude of coaches with regard to young athletes. One of the "transition" gymnasts reports:

> "The world championship was difficult because I was hurt, I felt a lot of pain, and there was [...] a lot of pressure, many unnecessary things."

Here she adds about the preparation for the Olympic Games:

> "[...] And I, emotionally speaking, I was very upset. As there was a lot of tension for a whole month preceding the Olympic Games, training alone in another country.
>
> I've always been very independent. I just arrived in another country and called: "Mom, I arrived and everything is okay". In the last day I called again: "Mom, I'm leaving here, I'll arrive in Brazil at such time", so that she could pick me up. In the middle of that month, then, I called my family more often, crying: "I'm tired!", I was just tired. I freely cried, I just couldn't avoid it. Thus, it was very overwhelming."

This gymnast didn't compete in the Olympic Games, since a stress fracture was detected in her leg and, certainly, this was a very negative experience for her and her coach, too. There has never been a conversation between them about what happened. This coaches' authority over the gymnasts led her to be unable to directly communicate with her coach and set her limits, something which ended up causing a severe injury, as earlier discussed by Mássimo (1996). The hard part is measuring the psychological injury caused in a situation like this.

Of course, this is only a partial view of the event, as the coaches' testimony isn't presented here, however, the literature addresses the emotional abuse on the part of coaches over child athletes. Gervis and Dunn (2004) conducted a study in the United Kingdom about the emotional abuse of elite child athletes by their coaches and they confirmed the lack of knowledge and/or adequate coaches' attitudes when dealing with children in sport. The results of this study aimed to make clear the behavior of some coaches as a threat to the psychological well-being of young elite athletes.

In AG, the specific modality characteristics themselves, such as, for instance, the requirement of accuracy and perfection in the execution of movements which, often, involve a risk to the gymnast's safety, they generate stress both in training sessions and in competitions. Regarding these experienced situations, some gymnasts discuss these moments and the way how they coped with these situations:

> *"Do you know why I won 1st place in the World Qualification Pre-Olympic tournament? My knee was hurt, I had a problem due to a little torsion, I had even undergone an intensive treatment with the doctors at [Universidade] Gama Filho, I had to take cortisone, I had to rest before achieving that. So, at the competition time, I wasn't worried about winning, being the 1st or 2nd place, qualifying for the Olympic Games, I was just concerned with making the wisest possible thing so that I didn't hurt myself, as well as I could overcome pain and the problems of not having trained as firmly as I wished. Thus, my concentration wasn't focused on fear of obtaining the qualification or not, but only on being kind to my little knee. I think that was the reason why I had some peace of mind with regard to the need for being invincible, and the top athletes, who were Lilian and Silvia, who were indicated as those having more chances to obtain the qualification, were tied with the same score just below me, in 2nd place. Funny, huh? That was a shock for everyone (laughs). They were from Tijuca, it was expected that one of them were qualified for the Olympic Games, and I was."*
>
> *"I stayed there for a year and a half. I stayed there until [19]83, when I managed to qualify for the Olympic Games. Then, I couldn't*

take it anymore, I came back to Brazil. Because the training session were very demanding at that time. I woke up at 5 o'clock, at 6 o'clock I was already training. For two periods. Then, I went school, went back, and practiced more. So... away from home... it all. I stayed there for a year and a half, then, I came back. When I came back, I just went to Flamengo, which was the best club at that time."

"It's very strict. And there's mechanization, repetition, and focus, focus, focus. But, well, at the same time we saw it was that way, it wasn't okay within me, I just couldn't take it so easily, without challenging anything. I think it shouldn't be this way. I really believe in mental training. A lot. There was a time when we had psychological support there, in Flamengo, and I attended the MDG course, i.e. "Mental Development and Guidance". At that time, it was widely used in the brazilian volleyball team, when Bernardinho was the coach. I think it may even relieve physical burden from some kind of training at some time. It doesn't mean replacing. It'll never replace physical training, but it's another kind of training which can constitute a very strong ally."

"I have all titles: "mirim", child, up to the adult category. Thus, I had already won all competitions I participated in. I was different from my father, as he was also involved in sport; his aim was gaining experience. Then, I was a 9-year old girl and he put me to compete in adult competitions. This way, I really had no success. But he always used to say: "no... it doesn't matter, the aim is gaining experience". I competed a lot. Yes, I dealt well with this because my daddy behaved this way, I remember this phrase very well. On the competition day, he said: "Look, go there and if you make everything wrong, there's no problem. I just want you to go, compete, so, you'll gain experience and slowly you'll become successful. Thus, there's no problem at all". So, today, I see the girls with their coaches. I spent a year and a half there, at the Excellence Center (Curitiba), and there's a stress similar to a competition, for them, competing involves a lot of adrenaline, that kind of thing. I didn't have it. I always competed in an easy way. I had an expectation of my own, I never liked to lose, to make mistakes. But this didn't come from the coach, never. It only happened when I was training at Flamengo. Very long afterwards. Neither at Pinheiros. It was very calm."

"I got very nervous. However, I was too controlled. I just knew that much later. I did my part. And, once, the assistant coach told me I was very lonely. Nobody talked to me, because they knew that was my way of focusing. They thought: that's her own way. She does her work. I was at such a high concentration level that I didn't see the competition happening. I knew my time, I just took a look to see which was my turn. But I stayed there, recalling the series in my head. I got stressed, but I knew how to focus, control. I remember I obtained a place in the podium in the two last championships I participated in, at both times I got on the balance beam, went to the podium, and, then, I thought: "oh... I think that's the last time I'm gonna do it. Why do I need to go through it?" I got very nervous! There was too much concentration so that I didn't get lost. There's a need for monitoring that nervousness all the time, so that I didn't get out of control."

"[...] Then, my concentration, my own way of focusing, changed; in 2000 I learned to focus in a way that I never thought of before, it was achieve along with my coach, she helped me, along with the Russian coach and she. Regarding concentration, I think it isn't possible to learn a lot, it only improves what you already have, so, I think the physical education professional has a lot of strength, because he is able to see it when the child is small. [...] So, in fact, they show that you just control yourself, then, if I don't know myself, he won't know me, because I'm the one who controls me."

"It was pretty cool in Athens, but it was very intense. It was a very tense stage in my life. Because there was expectation, an expectation from millions of people at the same time. Thus, it was something very stressful. My whole focus was there. In Athens, on the ground, especially because it was my best apparatus. It doesn't mean that I trained more on the ground, but my main focus was on the ground. But it was difficult. I think I lacked maturity! What led me to grow in gymnastics was the maturity I acquired. In order to deal with it all. It's hard to know how to deal with pressure, it's difficult to know how to cope with that, everything was there, on your hands. Because at that moment I had everything on my hands. It was this way: if you make no mistake at all, you'll be an Olympic champion. And it was a little step further I needed. It wasn't a lack of strength, but an excessive strength! Thus, I think it's maturity, something you gradually acquire over time. But that isn't enough! You acquire it during competitions. Only when you compete over and over again you acquire it. It isn't possible to transfer maturity from one person to another. Then, someone asked: "if you could go back, would you perform the same series?". I would! I would. However, if I had the awareness I have today, I'd control myself better than I did back then. So, in fact, it's a matter of lack of control which leads you to lose the medal."

"Nowadays, I don't get nervous when I compete. That year (2007) I got quite nervous. At all competitions I got nervous, I made mistakes on the balance beam, because I know it's my best apparatus and I knew I had a chance to win a medal in the Pan American Games. I knew that, perhaps, if I performed a series as I usually do in training sessions I could be there, or, in the final, or as a substitute athlete in the world championship final. Thus, it was a chance. I wasn't sad because mistakes happen, right? But I knew that if I stayed as calm as in all the other years when I competed on the beam, when I competed in a calm way, I could have been successful. So it's something I have to change, perhaps my concentration at that year on the beam wasn't as good as it was in other years. I need to see where I made a mistake there, because I know it's my best apparatus. And it's an apparatus where I do it very well, I know, nowadays, it's the apparatus where I have a chance. So, I was a little sad, because I saw that I could be in the final on the beam, at least as a substitute. And this is already a very difficult thing. But I relate well to this feature of the modality (accuracy), because I think the chances increase according to the way you train. Of course, you can't waste every opportunity you have, too. But it's a sport that... that wasn't my time, but if I change my concentration, if I focus very well, if I keep as calm as when I competed on the beam before, I know it's an apparatus where I'll have a chance."

"That competition (Olympic Games), for me, wasn't very good, because I competed only on the beam, I was very bad, I didn't like it. I performed 10 series (with no falls or imbalances) every day and just at that time something went wrong? I didn't like it at all. That sucks! I fell two or three times from the beam because I was extremely nervous, terrified, I had some nervous tics at the competition time and it was something inexplicable, because I performed 10 series with no mistake at all during the training sessions, everything was just okay. With my leg injured I was able to do that, I trained it. Oh! It happens, just as it happened to Daí (Daiane dos Santos), she made a mistake on the ground in the final, everyone may experience it!"

"We talked about all this pressure, because it's hard to be there, you have to train well, because there's always a referee looking at you, a coach watching you. And you can't cry, you can't pout. It was more difficult. If we cried, our coordinator was there, watching, and if we cried or pouted, she spoke about that. We knew we couldn't do that. It was a competition (the Olympic Games) at which I was... I wasn't as nervous as I thought I'd be. How people say, my coach and everyone else, say I'm, I seem to be the calmest girl. So, I always started in the apparatus, because I was the calmest one and I performed it more easily. There wasn't much trouble. And we started on the beam. I was the first one. So, I got very nervous, there was that huge gym, so *many people watching you. It can make us very nervous, but I was just fine."*

As mentioned in the theoretical basis of this research, these characteristics of the modality, besides providing the practitioners with pleasure, require a high concentration level from the gymnasts in order to be able to accurately perform its complex skills at the right time, i.e. during the competition.

Macneill (2007), studying the preparation of Canadian athletes who won Winter Olympic Games medals, in modalities such as skeleton and speed skating, found out in the interviews that the psychological work conducted considerably helped these athletes. Some of them attended meditation classes, other athletes analyzed for up to three consequent hours the various possibilities of their race, correcting and solving any kind of problems which could happen at the competition moment. One athlete approaches a holistic training plan that mixed physical and mental preparation for the Olympic Games days, such as: how to finish the race, how to stand out on the track, how to warm up, when a massage is needed, how to deal with the various distractions, and so on. The use of music was also included to help in terms of concentration before the races, even in the training sessions of athletes who weren't used to it, in order to isolate them from the attractive context of the Olympic Games.

Brandão (2005, p. 113), in this regard, comments that "the use of mental training seems essential to minimize or even eliminate the interference of negative psychological factors, in search of an excellent performance".

Another influence experienced by these female gymnasts, which was also a result of this rapid evolution, was the increased popularity of AG and, more specifically, of these gymnasts, who started gaining access to the mass media on a frequent basis, getting AG a little bit closer to the general public. The female gymnast from this generation who went through the apex of this popularity reports that:

> "Since this world championship (2003) my life has changed a lot. A lot (laughs)! This change was very difficult! It was very, very complicated because when we arrived at the world championship [...] I thought it would be like... I won another medal, just as anyone else. Because we weren't used to see that, at least me and everybody I knew."
>
> "When I arrived at the airport there were a lot of people. A lot! I came here by fire department truck, that whole thing. And I couldn't leave home, I couldn't even stay at home's gate, because there're people in front of my house all day long! So, for me, it was hard at first. It was a big reality shock. I think so. It happened overnight, indeed. So, I think it's something which scares us at first. And it isn't easy for getting used to. It takes a long time! It takes a long time for you to pick up the pace, understand the way how things would be from them on."
>
> "I deal very well with it. Not always! Because you have no privacy anymore. You go out dining in a restaurant and, one way or another, you're going to stop, everyone looks, you have to stop sometimes to give an autograph, take a photo. You need to have this kind of patience with people, because it's the retribution you give for the love they give you, too."

Another gymnast who also experienced this transition to the popularity of this modality, which probably started having greater intensity from the first medal won by Brazil in the World Qualification Pre-Olympic tournament of AG, when she was silver medalist:

> "2001, for me, was a year after the Olympic Games, we competed a Pan American in which I didn't performed that well, the adult Pan American, and, soon afterwards, a month, a month and a bit later, we were totally discredited, nobody knew what was gymnastics in Brazil, in a year I was very lucky, because football wasn't well, volleyball wasn't well, Guga wasn't well, so, it was a year in which Brazil was lacking athletes who stood out. And I won a medal, which was the first brazilian medal in the World Gymnastics Championship, something which was a great joy for me, being a blessed person, winning

the first medal. I just couldn't imagine the way how it would be when I arrived Brazil, because already there, in Ghent (Belgium), there were a lot of reporters calling me, the girls helped me to get ready, because soon after there would be the closing ceremony. There were reporters calling, the girls were helping me, the phone didn't stop, it didn't stop, and I think there was a great expectation for my arrival here, in Brazil."

"When I arrived, the person who was my adviser, who then was adviser at Flamengo, he spoke like this: "be not afraid, there're a few reporters". When he spoke of a few reporters, I believed, and thought like this: "Ah, there must be a few, indeed, because it's Gymnastics". When I came out of the arrival gate at the airport, I'd like to go back (laughs). There were a lot of people. A lot of people, many people, indeed."

"[...] Not now! Now, it's very different. We arrive at competitions, there's a need for safety, it's something we aren't used to, because I think when these competitions occur, people go because they want to see us close, because we became idols in our own country. So, sometimes I feel a little sad, because we can't meet all the children, because, for me, it's like this: an adult, if you say "hey... it isn't possible!", he understands, but how could we explain it to a child, that we can't provide her with attention at that moment? [...] So, it's something that an adult have patience, but a child hasn't it."

This popularity has its positive side, which values the practice of this modality, and, hence, there's a greater ease of financial support and dissemination of the modality itself, but it also logically increases pressure for a sport modality that has already pressure as a characteristic, both in training sessions, due to repetition and perfection, but in competitions, due to accuracy. One of the "new generation" gymnasts addresses this pressure on the gymnast Daiane dos Santos during the Olympic Games in Athens, where she competed for an Olympic medal:

"And that expectation was all over the poor girl, everyone was saying: Daiane will win! The girl's head was exploding. Then, that possibility didn't come true."

It was very different from the pioneering generation. One of the "pioneering gymnasts" reports in her testimony about the absence of brazilian supporters in the Moscow Olympic Games:

> "There, in Moscow, it was very beautiful! I trained, trained, trained in a day and competed in the other, trained, trained, trained in the other, and went on. I didn't watch João Luis[4], because he also didn't watch me, the day he competed, I was working very hard in the training sessions. There was no supporter, there was nobody from Brazil watching us, but I did everything right, I made no mistakes."

All these psychological aspects involved in the modality leads to a need for people with a particular psychological profile, who adapts or deal with these situations in a positive way, who channel them for overcoming and facing challenges, because, after all, the study approaches outstanding women artistic gymnasts, successful gymnasts. Arkaev and Suchilin (2004) advocate for the participation of the psychology professional in the modality when there's interest in performing psychological tests to outline the profile of champions and detect the same profile in children, something which is involved in the process of discovering and selecting talents in AG. According to Brandão (2005, p. 111):

> "A combination of factors contributes to the sport success: genetic predisposition, intensive training, and psychological qualities. Among them, primarily stands out a clear "mental picture" that the gymnast has about what she's looking for. One pays a very high price to achieve maximum performance and win competitions. Expectations are, generally, very high. There's a lot of pressure, one doesn't tolerate lack of effort and intensity and, daily, there's a high dose of tiredness. [...] We can say that the gymnast who effectively uses her mental strength develops great control over her emotions and has greater opportunities to compete in a flow (fluency) state. This state is related to a special feeling of confidence in her own possibilities and it makes you believe that everything will be alright. The gymnast

---

[4]Male gymnast representing Brazil in the same Olympic Games.

is focused, absorbed, and involved in the task and she doesn't notice anything around her, nothing can affect her."

Through the gymnasts' testimony, it was possible to realize that some manifestations may suggest certain gymnasts' characteristics, such as: determination, responsibility, discipline, focus, among others.

One of the "new generation" gymnasts deals well with pressures and shows to be very calm during competitions, she usually starts in each apparatus[5], as previously mentioned in her testimony. Another gymnast in the same group also deals well with pressures of this modality, the strictness of coaches and training sessions, distance from family, being one of the few gymnasts who don't talk of suffering or major complaints with regard to her career. This gymnast reports her strategies for dealing with the Ukrainian coaches' commitment and the strong pace in training sessions:

"Regarding the training session with the Ukrainians, I'm humored. So, I always try to smile, I'm always telling a joke, something like that. Sometimes, the training session is very hard, everyone with that face, [...] and, then, I try doing some little thing for getting better, because this way the training sessions leads to better results, and you get more willing to practice. Because they're much colder. Oh, my! Much colder! To make them laughing at this this gym, one has to... I really don't know."

One of the "pioneering" gymnasts also has a similar profile to that gymnast who reports the coldness of Ukrainian coaches, she shows to be more relaxed, she doesn't get easily emotionally upset and her testimony doesn't report suffering, rather, she often speaks of pleasure in gymnastics.

"When my family, for instance, went on vacation to travel or know the Northeast, my sister, my father, my mother, tourism, indeed, I

---

[5] Usually, the coaches tend to put a confident gymnast to start the team's participation in each apparatus, aiming to obtain a good team's impression before the referees.

didn't allowed them to take me. When they took me and I had to miss the weekend or five days to go on vacation with them, I'd be the most unhappy person in the world. So, I slept at Altair's home, I slept with my friends, with another friend, Andréia, but they were traveling and I stayed here. Always!"

The gymnasts' responsibility is also a common feature which is reflected not only in gymnastics, but in other contexts of their lives:

"And I was very responsible, if I had to study I woke up at 5 a.m., because at night I couldn't, I just fainted when I came home. When I sat on the couch and I slept. But if I had to study for a test, or something like this, I woke up early, studied, and went on. So, the support came from everyone. In the gym everyone was supporting each other."

"I completed college at the usual time and I didn't fail any subject, I never had to do any additional test. I've always been a good student, from school, I've never had a red mark. It depends on the person's personality, not just at the gym, but at the school and anywhere, and one of the reasons why my father allowed me keep practicing gymnastics, in the beginning, was getting good marks at school. So, if I was doing bad at school he'd get me out of gymnastics, then, I paid much attention at school to compensate, because I had no time to study."

Other common features among gymnasts are independence and determination, as a "new generation" gymnast reports:

"Oh! I think what the team has in common is always wanting to do better than the other one. We always want to do the best in order to be able to get a better place. I think everybody has it, the pluck and the will to want that."

"It's something that everybody dreams of: "I want to go to the Olympic Games", for me, it was impossible. So, gradually, it came true. When I started traveling, for the first championships, I said: "it can't be possible!". But you need to have a lot of dedication, a lot of effort, I knew that the pathway wasn't by the sea, there was stone, but if that was what I wanted, so I said: "I want it!"."

"I had these clear targets. As I wasn't in any apparatus, I was a regular gymnast, so, my goal was to be in this pattern, so, I intended to be

at an Olympic final, then, I started training from there, for four more years. I've been perfecting myself on the parallel, on the beam, on the ground, on the jump, in order to keep that average and achieve my goal. So, everything was planned, I wasn't "at the final by chance", it had always been my goal. I prepared myself psychologically to reach an Olympic final."

"And I, not me[6], I want it ! I want, want, want, want. A very stubborn thing, indeed. Then, I went back and started training all over again, I kept training."

"In the training sessions, I'm usually always good humored. It's hard for me to be sulk. When I'm in a bad mood, it's visible on my face. But it's very hard for me to be sulk. Usually, I'm always humored."

"But I relate well with this feature of the modality (accuracy), because I think that the more you train, the more opportunities you have. Of course, every opportunity you have, you can't waste it, too. But it's a sport which... it wasn't this time, but if I change my concentration, if I focus on well, if I keep calm as I competed on the beam before, I know it's an apparatus in which I'll have a chance."

"In the very championship, I knew about the qualification for the Olympic Games. I knew if I made no mistakes in the competitions I'd qualify for the competition. And I can't explain. Because it was something already expected. Within me, it was like this: "I have to do what I have to do". I never even thought of the possibility of failing to go. It never went through my mind, failing to qualify. This championship was the pinnacle of my life; I'd participate and, then, I was going to see how I'd finish my career."

"[...] "Wow, I want to stop", no, but I'll regret. How am I going to see myself? I struggled all this time. No, my goal is the Olympic Games."

"And it was funny, too, the first international trip. All the other girls' mothers worried because the daughters would be traveling alone at 11 years of age. And my mother was almost laughing, because I had already decided who would sit by my side on the plane. I didn't care if I was traveling without my mom or not, do you understand? I was all happy because I was traveling with the group. I remember her commenting that to me, that mothers were worried about leaving their children and she hadn't this concern because she saw that I'd be pretty confident there, on that trip."

---

[6]Reaction after participating as a substitute in the Olympic Games in Sydney (2000) and return to training sessions, while other gymnasts who also failed to qualify stopped training.

The introspection, going back towards yourself, is also a prominent feature highlighted both by Smoleuskiy and Gaverdouskiy (1996) and João and Fernandes Filho (2002), as one of the "transition gymnasts" comments:

> "Because it was a characteristic of mine, I was very individualistic. I knew about my stuff only. I didn't see much, I saw what the girls told, the results, I looked and there was a big difference from my first score to the second one. Then, I compared myself more to the other girls from other countries who were also trying to qualify."

The outstanding characteristics of gymnasts, interpreted through their testimony, involving responsibility, determination, not being easily emotionally shaken, the perseverance to keep looking for new challenges and overruns, independence, to be more introverted than extroverted, and confidence corroborate data from the literature. According to Smoleuskiy and Gaverdouskiy (1996), the main features of gymnasts are: accuracy and emotional stability, high mastery and volitional ability, highly developed concentration abilities and alertness during the movements, and focusing on to the point of "disconnecting" from undesirable outside situations. João and Fernandes Filho (2002), in a study with outstanding brazilian athletes, found out low responses with regard to general degrees of emotional sensitivity and high average on affirmation tests.

Bortoleto (2004), in an observation of the main male Spanish artistic gymnasts for a year and a half, reports that one of the observed features was patience, due to the difficulty in visualizing the long-term goals. "The nature of training also requires a high discipline capacity, compliance with rules, and, why not, 'submission' to a strict and systematic teaching, based on repetition and obedience to the coaches' orders" (Bortoleto, 2004, p. 407). Moreover, the same author also highlights the courage and bravery, related both to many challenging exercises and to coping with the difficult situations which emerge from training sessions.

Tani, Teixeira, and Ferraz (1994), quoted by Simões, Böhme, and Lucato (1999), pointed out that some concerns call the attention of relatives, scholars, and researchers of the child within competitive sport, especially the aspects related to the formation and development of child's personality. These authors also address the issue of transfer of social behaviors acquired, encouraged, or constructed in the sport life, saying that many people believe that child competitiveness is taken to the individuals' social life, while others believe that the dedication, discipline, and cooperation developed in sport contribute to the children's training.

Regarding the psychological aspects reported in the gymnasts' testimonies in this research, one realizes that, despite all the stressful situations experienced by gymnasts, the response is positive when weighing the positive and negative points of the modality, with a "worthwhile" sensation.

> "You know, girls see training sessions as a punishment, suffering. "Wow! We train seven hours a day! Wow! Sometimes, there's no weekend". I think nothing will be a suffering if it pleases you to do. Gymnastics is something which is impossible to do if you don't like it. If you have no pleasure, you have no way to spend seven hours every day training, without enjoying it. So, for people, I abdicated so many years of my life, 13 years of my life, to gymnastics, abdicated from being with my family, having a boyfriend, getting married, having children. I don't see this way, because, on the other hand, because of that I was world champion, I went to other countries, I know a lot of people, I have many diplomas, a lot of decorations. Almost no one has it. So, it's like this: everything in life requires you to give up something to gain another one. If I had to do it all again, I would. I would! There would be no problem at all. Because I don't regret having trained all I trained, giving up so many things."
>
> "I'm on gymnastics for 19 years. I think what keeps me involved for so long is pleasure, because, in fact, I know that sponsorship is

meant to provide me with a structure, to provide me with a support, but there's no money which makes me stay from the moment I say "I don't want anymore". I'm still on gymnastics not for the money. Money is important, indeed. But if you do something just because it's a duty, it starts losing that taste. The, you can't stay, you could stay for 20 years, but you end up staying for 10 years. So, it's really what I like to do, gymnastics."

"The good side of gymnastics, I think, is traveling around the world. In my first trip abroad I was 12 years old, and I went alone. We went for training, I did an exchange, I stayed one month training in the USA, but my first competition was the Pan American Championship [...] in Colombia. So, you learn and experience many different cultures, learn how to deal with money, with different currencies, different people, different languages, you have some notion. Today, they speak to me: how many languages do you speak? I don't know, but I'm able to be by myself anywhere in the world."

"I think that when I have children... oh, I don't know. I think I'll enroll in AG. I'll enroll. If she's able, if I realize that she's able. If she's able and wants to, she'll train. And I'll endeavor so that she goes on if she wants to stop. But then, I don't know, I didn't think much about it. Because it's really very painful, but there's always the good side. Yes... there has to be the good side. I had many joys. Many. It's what I told you in the beginning, I'm very proud of everything I accomplished, of what I experienced... and there's a luggage like this. Many things I apply to my life. This responsibility issue, avoid giving up."

Perhaps a way to check that the balance of this experience was really positive is that, out of the seven already retired gymnasts, five became professional AG teachers after the end of their sport career, one works with fitness in gyms, but she dreams of having an AG gym, the another one is an artist at Cirque du Soleil and intends to become a coach on the modality in the future.

11.4 Final remarks

There's no previous record on this issue on brazilian athletes with such details, which are characteristic of the research type and the method chosen, therefore, these data provide a significant contribution as a reflection for coaches, psychologists, and other professionals involved in sport, in addition to the possibility of generating other surveys to lead this investigation type further.

Through the cross-analysis, one found out in the "pioneering" gymnasts' generation that there wasn't enough or continued support from sport psychology professionals. And, when there was some, it was occasional and not continued. Among "transition gymnasts" and the "new generation", there was psychological support only when the training sessions were transferred to the AG Excellence Center, where, since the Olympic Games in Sydney (2000), there's a multidisciplinary team to follow-up the preparation of the gymnasts from the permanent AG national team. One of the "transition" gymnasts didn't experience this ongoing selection period in the Excellence Center and she had no psychological monitoring, even after a stress injury which took her out of the Olympic Games, just on their eve.

The culture of not being able to freely speak to the coaches has been cultivated in gyms, as well as a childish treatment towards female gymnasts in the adult category, who start their training sessions in childhood and remain with the same relation to their coaches throughout their sport careers. These two factors together can generate an insurmountable barrier and a threat to the psychological well-being of young elite athletes, and even compromise their results.

Both testimonies and the literature report that, often, the coaches themselves end up conducting the "psychological work" along with the gymnasts, due to lack of structure or financial resources for hiring a professional or by choice, because they believe to know better each athlete. However, one emphasizes, based on the discussion in this chapter, that coaches, many times, can't handle the situations emerging from training sessions and competitions, as they're excessively involved in the context, due to lack of training for such intervention or lack of a professional look.

The testimonies presented in this chapter may not portray the brazilian reality as a whole, therefore, they can't be generalized. However, they represent the conditions of the ten most outstanding female gymnasts in Brazil from 1980 to 2004, from their own perspective, providing the sport professionals with reflections related to the directions in artistic gymnastics, so that it can be an excellence modality in Brazil not only with regard to the results, but to the process adopted for training the gymnasts.

References

Arkaev, L. I., & Suchilin, N.G. (2004). *Gymnastics: how to create champions*. Oxford: Meyer & Meyer Sport.

Benk, R. T. (2006). *Retreinamento das atribuições de sucesso e fracasso no esporte: uma proposta de intervenção pedagógica*. (Doctoral dissertation). Faculdade de Ciências da Saúde, Universidade de Brasília, Brasília.

Bortoleto, M. A. C. (2004). *La lógica interna de la gimnasia artística masculina (GAM) y estudio etnográfico de un gimnasio de alto redimiento*. (Doctoral dissertation). Instituto Nacional de Educación Física, Universitat de Lleida, Lleida.

Brandão, M. R. F. (2005). Aspectos psicológicos da Ginástica Artística. In M. Nunomura, & V. L. Nista-Piccolo (Eds.), *Compreendendo a ginástica artística* (pp. 107-117). São Paulo: Phorte.

Gervis, M., & Dunn, N. (2004). The emotional abuse of elite child athletes by their coaches. *Child Abuse Review, 13*, 215-223.

João, A., & Fernandes Filho, J. (2002). Identificação do perfil genético, somatotípico e psicológico das atletas brasileiras de ginástica olímpica feminina de alta qualificação esportiva. *Fitness & Performance, 1*(2), 12-20.

Macneill, K. C. (2007). *Processes contributing to optimal preparation and performance of winter olimpic athletes: the athletes's story*. (Doctoral dissertation). The Faculty of British Columbia, Otawa, Canada.

Mássimo, J. (1996). Psychology and safety in gymnastics. *Technique, 16*(6), 1-3.

Meihy, J. C. S. B. (2005). *Manual de história oral (5a. ed.)*. São Paulo: edições Loyola.

Queiroz, M. I. P. (1988). Relatos orais: do indivizível ao "divizível". In O. R. M. von Simson (Ed.), *Experimentos com histórias de vida: Itália-Brasil* (pp. 14-43). São Paulo: Vértice.

Schiavon, L. M. (2009). *Ginástica Artística feminina e História Oral: a formação desportiva de atletas brasileiras participantes de Jogos Olímpicos (1980-2004)*. (Doctoral dissertation). Faculdade de Educação Física, Universidade Estadual de Campinas, Campinas-SP. Last retrieved on July 31, 2012 from: http://cutter.unicamp.br/document/?code=000439200.

Simões, A. C., Böhme, M. T. S., & Lucato, S. (1999). A participação dos pais na vida esportiva dos filhos. *Revista Paulista de Educação Física, 13*(1), 34-45.

Simson, O. R. M. (1988). *Experimentos com histórias de vida*. Revista dos Tribunais e Vértices. São Paulo: Vértice - Editora Revista dos Tribunais.

Smoleuskiy, V., & Gaverdouskiy, I. (1996). *Tratado general de gimnasia artística deportiva*. Barcelona: Paidotribo.

Thompson, P. (2002). *História oral: a voz do passado (3a. ed)*. Rio de Janeiro: Paz e Terra.

Williams, K., & Warkov, A. (1995). Girl talk. *Women's Sports and Fitness, 17*(1), 32-37.

Author's biographies (in alphabetical order)

Kizzy Fernandes Antualpa. Kizzy is a doctoral student of University of São Paulo (USP). She studies and researches various factors concerning organization, structure, monitoring, and adaptation responses resulting from training processes. She is a lecturer in physical education at Metrocamp / Ibmec, as well as a coordinator and coach of the rhythmic gymnastics team.

Maria de Lurdes Tristão Ávila-Carvalho. Maria is an invited auxiliary professor in the Sports Faculty at Porto University. She holds a master's degree in sports sciences, specializing in high performance sports training in gymnastics. Her PhD in sports sciences focused on high level training in rhythmic gymnastics. She is an international rhythmic gymnastics judge. Maria has published articles in international journals, book chapters, and she took part in international congresses.

Mélix Ilisástigui Avilés. Mélix is a vice rector of the UCCFD "Manuel Fajardo", Cuba. She is the head of the national technical commission of rhythmic gymnastics, and a regular professor of the UCCFD "Manuel Fajardo" with 32 years of experience in education. She received a PhD in pedagogic sciences and holds a master's degree in methodology of sports training focusing on rhythmic gymnastics. She acts as an international judge in RG since 1987. She is a member of the national technical commission, of the scientific advice committee of the UCCFD, and of the permanent tribunal of scientific degrees of sciences of the physical culture. She is furthermore a member of the doctoral committee of her university, and of the academic committee of the program of master of methodology of the training for the high competition. Additionally she is a member of the master's program committee of psychology in sport. She acts as a coordinator and professor of the graduate degree specialising in high performance in rhythmic gymnastics.

Nelly Ochoa Borrás. Nelly is a teacher and instructor of the Department of Physical Education of the University of Sciences of the Physical Culture "Manuel Fajardo" (Cuba). She holds a master's degree in methodology of sports training. She was a former gymnast of the national preselection and coach of the national selection of group of rhythmic gymnastics for more than 10 years. For more than 5 years she acted as a manager of the cuban national selection. She is a member of the national technical commission of rhythmic gymnastics, and she is a professor of the graduate degree focusing on high performance in rhythmic gymnastics.

Marco Antonio Coelho Bortoleto. Marco graduated in physical education at Methodist University of Piracicaba (Brazil). He holds a master's degree in physical education from University of Campinas (Brazil), and he received his PhD from the national Institute of Physical Education of Catalonia of the University of Lleida (Spain). He currently works as an assistant professor at the Physical Education Faculty of the University of Campinas (UNICAMP).

Ivan Čuk. Ivan served as a PE teacher, coach, international judge, FIG consultant, researcher, television commentator, manager, publisher, and university professor. He signed 59 scientific articles and 22 books. Most known books are with Istvan Karacsony on pommel horse exercises, rings, vault, and floor exercises. He established the Science of Gymnastics Journal (www.scienceofgymnastics.com) to join science and practice of all gymnastics disciplines. Today he works at the Faculty of Sport, University of Ljubljana, as chief of the gymnastics department and the department of kinesiology. His last big achievement was his exhibition at Slovenian National Gallery with celebration of 150 years of gymnastics in Slovenia.

Yolaini Govea Díaz. Yolaini is an assisting professor of the Physical Culture Nancy Uranga of Pinegrove of the River, of the University of Sciences of the Physical Culture "Manuel Fajardo" (UCCFD), Cuba, with 10 years of experience. She received a PhD in sciences of the physical culture. She is a member of the technical commission of rhythmic gymnastics. She was a former gymnast of rhythmic gymnastics, and she is now a professor of the graduate degree focusing in high performance in rhythmic gymnastics.

César Jose Duarte Peixoto. César is a member of the National Gymnastics federation, and president of the scientific committee. He studied at Lisbon University. His main research interests are in the field of coaching methodology and movement analyses in gymnastics.

Author's biographies.

Hardy Fink. Hardy has been Director of FIG Education and Academy Programs since 2005 and was involved in that program from the very first meetings in 1995. He has expanded the program to include all disciplines in more than 160 academies since he began in his current position and has recently produced a men's and women's Age Group Development and Competition Program that has been introduced world-wide in the past three years. He was ten years Canada's men's National Coach and High Performance Director and also Men's Program Director. Before that he was a successful private club owner and placed both men and women on Canada's national teams. He taught biomechanics and coaching science at the University of British Colombia for five years and was a member of FIG's Men's Technical Committee for sixteen years, including four years as president.

Thomas Heinen. Thomas studied sport science and psychology. He is a trained sport psychologist and sport physiotherapist and he holds the FIG level III coaching license for women's artistic gymnastics. He earned a PhD from the German Sport University Cologne in 2006 (major topic: psychology). In 2013 he received his postdoctoral lecture qualification in sport science, and he currently works as a professor of social sciences of sport at the Institute of Sport Science of the University of Hildesheim (Germany). He is a member of the scientific commission of the FIG.

Gareth Irwin. Gareth is a professor and the head of sports biomechanics at the Cardiff School of Sport, Cardiff Metropolitan University. Gareth has two main research interest, coaching biomechanics interface, and sports medicine and injury. As a former international gymnast and national coach his research is informed by a rich experiential background. Gareth is a fellow and vice president of the International Society of Biomechanics in Sport. He has over 130 peer-reviewed publications including book chapters, papers and conference articles, and has delivered 30 national and international invited presentations. Gareth is also a consultant for the International Gymnastics Federation science commission.

David Kerwin. David is professor emeritus of biomechanics in the School of Sport at Cardiff Metropolitan University in the UK. He is a fellow of ISBS, the British Association of Sport and Exercises Sciences and the Royal Society of Medicine. He is a member of the peer review college for the Engineering and Physical Sciences Research Council in the UK. David has been part of the International Olympic Medical Commission's research team at four Summer Olympic Games, and a member of the International Gymnastics Federation science commission. He specialises in understanding human movements in athletics, gymnastics, and soccer. David has published over 200 papers in journals and conferences and supervised more than 20 PhD students.

Eunice Lebre. Eunice is a sports manager in the FIG. She is an expert of rhythmic gymnastics in the FIG Coaches Education Academies. She holds a PhD in sports sciences focusing on training in high level performance for gymnastics. She was a teacher (1987-2012) in the Sport Faculty in the Oporto University. Her publications cover articles in international journals, book chapters and contributions to international Congresses. She acts as a reviewer for international journals.

Márcia Regina Aversani Lourenço. Márcia is a graduate associate in physical education at UEM/UEL. She holds a master's degree in pedagogy from the Methodist University of Piracicaba. She is furthermore licensed in physical education by the Faculty of Physical Education of Northern Paraná. She is a coordinator of the physical education and specialization in rhythmic gymnastics, and a professor of the professional masters program in physical exercise in health promotion from the University of Northern Paraná (UNOPAR). She is an international judge of rhythmic gymnastics.

Myrian Nunomura. Myrian is an associate professor at the School of Physical Education and Sport, University of São Paulo, Brazil (since 1996). She completed a post-doctorate fellowship at University of Tsukuba (2004-2005; 2006-2008). She received her PhD in sports sciences from the State University of Campinas (1998-2001), her master's degree in education from Yokohama National University (1992-1995), and she holds a bachelor's degree in physical education (1986-1989). She was a former artistic gymnastics coach and FIG judge, as well as a preschool and elementary school physical education teacher.

Mauricio Santos Oliveira. Maurico was a former gymnast and coach. He graduated at Gymnastikhoejskolen i Ollerup in Denmark. He holds a bachelor's degree in physical education, a bachelor's degree in sport of physical education, and a master's degree in physical education (State University of Campinas, Brazil). Currently he is developing a PhD project at the School of Physical Education and

Sport at the University of São Paulo, Brazil. He is also an assistant professor at the Federal University of Espírito Santo, Brazil.

Ieda Parra Barbosa Rinaldi. Ieda received her master's degree and her PhD from the Faculty of Physical Education at Unicamp. She is licensed in physical education by the Department of Physical Education of the State University of Maringá. She is furthermore a professor at the Department of Physical Education of the State University of Maringá and a program graduate associate in physical education at UEM/UEL. She leads the research group gymnastics: training, intervention and school of DEF/UEM.

Jean-François Robin Jean-François was a former gymnastics coach during the last 15 years, and a researcher of the Paris East University for 12 years. He currently works as the deputy head of the Research Department, and as the deputy director of the Laboratory of Sport, Expertise and Performance to the French National Institute of Sports (INSEP).

Keith Russell. Keith is a professor in the College of Kinesiology, University of Saskatchewan, Canada. He was a former canadian men's national gymnastics coach, being canadian male coach of the Year in 1995 (individual sports). He has received the Geoff Gowan Award for Lifetime Achievement in 2010 from the Coaching Association of Canada. He is the president of the FIG scientific commission as of 2009 and member of Writing Groups for FIG Coach Education Academies level 1, 2 & 3 for: artistic, trampoline, acrobatic, and gymnastics-for-all.

Laurita Marconi Schiavon. Laurita is an assistant professor at the Physical Education Department of the São Paulo State University (UNESP, Rio Claro, São Paulo, Brazil). She graduated, received a master's degree, and her PhD in physical education from the University of Campinas (São Paulo, Brazil). She acts as an international women's artistic gymnastics judge. Her research interests are: sport pedagogy and gymnastics pedagogy. She is a coordinator of the gymnastics research group at UNESP.

Catarina Paula Leandro Sousa e Silva. Catarina finished her master's degree in sport for children and youngsters in the University of Porto in 2009. She is a teacher at the Lusófona University. She belongs to the Judging Council of the FGP and she is an international rhythmic gymnastics judge of the FIG with functions in World Cups, European and World Championships. She published chapters in published books and technical production. In her professional activities she has interacted with collaborators in the co-authorship of scientific papers.

Eliana de Toledo Eliana has a degree in physical education, and she is undergraduated in sports training. She has a master's degree in physical education from UNICAMP and a PhD in history from Pontifícia Universidade Católica de São Paulo (PUCSP). Her involvement in the field of gymnastics is vast: she was an athlete, acted as a coach and referee, was a member of the São Paulo Committee Federation and a university teacher (in the undergraduate and post-graduate courses). Currently she is a professor of the sports science course in the Applied Sciences College (FCA - Faculdade de Ciências Aplicadas at UNICAMP/Limeira). She furthermore is a coordinator of the Laboratory of Research and Experiences in Gymnastics (LAPEGI at FCA/UNICAMP), and a member of the Group of Research in Gymnastics at the Faculty of Physical Education/UNICAMP and director of GÍMNICA – Gymnastics Virtual Library (www.gimnica.com).

Konstantinos Velentzas. Konstantinos studied sport science at the University of Athens. He is a trained sport psychologist and he holds the coaching licence of the German Volleyball Federation (A-Level). He worked as an assistant coach and sport psychologist with the women's national volleyball team (U18). He earned a PhD from the German Sport University Cologne in 2010 (major topic: psychology). Kostas currently works as a lecturer at the Department of Sport Science at the University of Bielefeld (Germany).

Pia Maria Vinken. Pia studied sport science at the German Sport University in Cologne. Furthermore Pia is a trained sport psychologist, sport physiotherapist, (personal) fitness trainer, and she holds a national woman's artistic gymnastics coaching license (B-level). Since 2007, Pia assisted in several research projects concerning sport science, psychology and gymnastics as a research assistant and scientific coworker. From 2011 she had several lecturer positions at the Leibniz University Hanover, the German Sport University Cologne and the University of Hildesheim (Germany). She is currently finishing her PhD thesis, dealing with a topic that could be relevant for all areas of gymnastics.

Author's biographies.

Geneviève Williams. Geneviève is a post doctoral researcher in biomechanics and motor control at The Pennsylvania State University, University of Massachusetts, and Cardiff Metropolitan University. Her research is focused on understanding complex systems and applying them to an ecologically valid sporting environment. Geneviève is unique in her exploration of the interface between motor control and the biophysical aspects of human performance. Geneviève is an internationally recognized researcher and a regular presenter at national and international conferences. She has published in a number of books, abstracts, and peer review papers in prestigious journals.